trees

An **EXPLORE
YOUR WORLD**™
Handbook

DISCOVERY COMMUNICATIONS, INC., produces high-quality television programming, interactive media, books, films, and consumer products. DISCOVERY NETWORKS, a division of Discovery Communications, Inc., operates and manages the Discovery Channel, TLC, Animal Planet, Travel Channel, and the Discovery Health Channel.

Trees, An Explore Your World ™ Handbook, was created and produced by ST. REMY MEDIA INC.

Library of Congress Cataloging-in-Publication Data
Arno, Jon
　Trees : an Explore your world handbook /
　　[Jon Arno, consultant] — 1st ed.
　　　p. cm.
　Includes bibliographical references (p.).
　ISBN 1-56331-840-7
　　1. Trees—Handbooks, manuals, etc. 2. Trees--
　Identification--Handbooks, manuals, etc.
　　I. Title.

　QK475　A27 2000
　582.16—dc21
　　　　　　　　　　　　　　　　　　　　　　00-029449

CONSULTANTS

Jon Arno is a writer and consultant specializing in wood technology and the properties, sources, and uses of commercial timbers. Arno is the author of *The Woodworker's Visual Handbook* (Rodale, 1995) and numerous articles for popular publications, such as *Fine Woodworking* magazine and *Woodshop News.* He also provided technical editing support for the Time-Life series *The Art of Woodworking* and the USDA-Forest Products Laboratory's *Wood Handbook.* A graduate of the University of Michigan, Arno currently resides in Troy, Michigan.

James Flynn, Jr. is a retired operations research analyst who now serves as associate editor of *World of Wood,* the journal of the International Wood Collectors Society, for which he also writes a monthly column, "Wood of the Month." Flynn has authored columns on dendrochronology, musical wood, and field collecting wood. He has also published *A Guide to Useful Woods of the World* and authored the book *Building the Balaika.*

Jim Fyles is an Associate Professor of Forest Science in the Department of Natural Resource Sciences at the Macdonald Campus of McGill University in Ste Anne de Bellevue, Quebec, Canada. He is Director of the Molson Nature Reserve in southern Quebec and past Associate Director of the McGill School of Environment.

Todd Forrest is Curator of Woody Plants at the New York Botanical Garden in the Bronx. He has worked in the curatorial department at the Arnold Arboretum of Harvard University. He received a Masters of Forest Science at Yale University.

Dr. Jeff Kirwan has spent thirty years educating youth about forestry and natural resources. He currently serves as Virginia Tech's Extension Specialist for Natural Resources Education. He has also worked as a 4-H Extension Agent and a biology teacher. His research interests include forest ecology, ecosystems, and land-use change.

trees

An **EXPLORE
YOUR WORLD**™
Handbook

DISCOVERY BOOKS
NEW YORK

CONTENTS

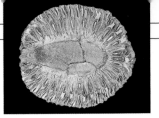

THE LIFE OF A TREE

THE WORLD OF TREES

*A world without trees? Not only would it be a world
greatly diminished in beauty, it would also be one where
life wouldn't exist as we know it today.*

It's easy to take trees for granted. They're a familiar part of almost every landscape on the planet. But they are also highly sophisticated organisms that have endured and adapted through millions of years of evolution. And beyond their complex design, trees contribute to life on Earth in countless ways. They clean and oxygenate the air, prevent soil erosion, and help keep the atmosphere at a livable temperature. And that's just the beginning. Trees provide animals and humans alike with food and shelter, and are a source of other important resources, such as fuel and lumber. In fact, the very course of human history has been strongly influenced by trees—and wood in particular—with the development of everything from spears to ships.

The flattened tops of an acacia (Acacia) are a familiar sight on the savanna of the African plains. The distinctive shape is the result of giraffes browsing on the tree's leaves.

Botanists have identified about a hundred thousand tree species—about twice the number of vertebrate animal species on the planet. Before human beings began cutting down forests for lumber and to make room for agriculture, forests covered a wide range of terrestrial environments. This extraordinary level of success reflects the remarkable adaptations that allow trees to thrive in unlikely places. Species found in deserts and arid lands typically survive long periods of drought by hoarding moisture. The impressively bulbous baobab tree (*Adansonia digitata*) shrinks noticeably in size during droughts in its African habitat as its water reserves are put to use. Other tree species can grow high up on wind-blown mountainsides with little more than rock to support their roots. Often such trees survive by

A walker out for a morning stroll is dwarfed by the majestic forms of sequoias (Sequoiadendron giganteum) in Sequoia National Park, California. The bark of sequoias is thick and contains no resin, making the trees very resilient against forest fires.

growing extremely slowly and remaining very small. Some of the stunted, weathered bristlecone pines (*Pinus longaeva*) in California sprouted more than 4,500 years ago, before the pyramids were built. In fact, trees are the oldest living organisms on the planet—as well as the largest. There are coast redwoods (*Sequoia sempervirens*) that tower more than 350 feet (110 m) high, while massive sequoias (*Sequoiadendron giganteum*) can weigh in at more than one thousand tons.

Whatever their size or shape, each species of tree functions not only as a highly resilient soldier in the plant kingdom's array of colonial forces, but also as part of a complex interdependent collection of life forms populating the world's various biomes. Each biome, whether it be a tropical rain forest, a northern boreal forest, or an arid chaparral, represents a unique ecological community.

The various communities are profiled at the back of this book as a framework for looking at more than 160 of the most interesting and representative species of trees from around the world *(pages 84 to 175)*.

> *"The tree which moves some to tears of Joy is in the Eyes of others only a Green thing that stands in their way. Some see Nature all Ridicule & Deformity . . . and some scarce see Nature at all. But to the Eyes of the Man of Imagination, Nature is Imagination itself."*
>
> — WILLIAM BLAKE (1757-1827)

CLASSIFYING TREES

A distinction is often made—particularly in temperate climates, where mixed forests are common—between coniferous, needle-bearing trees and broad-leaved, deciduous trees. Conifers are commonly known as evergreens because of a popular impression that all such trees keep their needles throughout the year, unlike deciduous trees, which shed leaves in autumn. However, some conifers, such as the bald cypress (*Taxodium distichum*), do in fact shed their needles, and many tropical and temperate broad-leaved trees are designated as evergreens by botanists because they replace their leaves gradually over time. To add to the confusion, certain broad-leaved trees, such as the ginkgo (*Ginkgo biloba*), are more closely related to conifers than to other broad-leaved trees.

A Tree by Any Other Name

Throughout this book, the common names of trees are accompanied by Latin equivalents used in a hierarchical system of classification that was created by Swedish botanist Carolus Linnaeus in the eighteenth century. The Linnaean system divides the plant kingdom into successively smaller, more exclusive groups, including families, genera, and species. Accordingly, each plant is assigned a generic and a specific name. Take shagbark hickory, for example. It has also been given the scientific name *Carya ovata*. The generic word *Carya* identifies it as being a member of the genus hickory—one of six genera in the walnut family Juglandaceae—while the epithet *ovata* tells us precisely what species of hickory it is.

Exposed to the elements on its isolated perch, a Jeffrey pine (Pinus jeffreyi) in California's Yosemite National Park serves as a visual testament to the power of prevailing winds.

The lush temperate rain forest in New England National Park in Australia is dominated by Antarctic beech (Nothofagus moorei). Rain forests boast the most diversified collection of flora and fauna on the planet, and can be found in areas from the northwestern coast of North America to central South America and Asia.

Trees are more accurately divided into two main groups, angiosperms and gymnosperms, according to the way they produce and present their seeds *(page 14)*. There are less than one thousand species of gymnosperms. Most of them are conifers, an ancient lineage of trees that is well adapted to life in cold, dry, and windy climates. Huge conifer forests cover much of the northern hemisphere and more of the world's surface than any other forest type. However, as the planet's climate becomes warmer, deciduous trees are pushing farther north.

Angiosperm species are typically broad-leaved, deciduous trees and are often referred to as hardwoods. Gymnosperm species are called softwoods, but these terms can be misleading. While lumber from angiosperms does tend to be heavier and harder, there are many exceptions. For example, balsa (*Ochroma pyramidale*) is an angiosperm species, but it has very soft, light wood. Many southern United States yellow pines, such as longleaf pine (*Pinus palustris*), are gymnosperms, but produce woods that are much stronger and heavier than such angiosperm species as American basswood (*Tilia americana*) and black walnut (*Juglans nigra*).

The more crucial difference between the woods of angiosperms and gymnosperms is the means by which trees in each group transport water from roots to leaves *(page 35)*. Advanced angiosperms have evolved much larger and more efficient vessels to handle the task. As a result, hardwoods are more complex in appearance, making their woods easy to distinguish from softwoods.

The Dawn of the Modern Forest

When plant life began in the sea billions of years ago, Earth's surface was inhospitable. The atmosphere was made up largely of carbon dioxide and methane, and the sun's ultraviolet rays bombarded the upper atmosphere that filtered the sun's ultraviolet rays. This protection allowed oxygen to accumulate below and created a surface environment where plants—and eventually animals—could live.

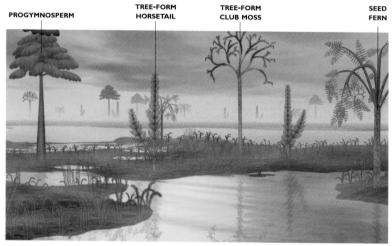

PROGYMNOSPERM   TREE-FORM HORSETAIL   TREE-FORM CLUB MOSS   SEED FERN

A Forest Scene—350 Million Years Ago
At the dawn of the Carboniferous, plants began to attain treelike stature. In this progenitor of modern forests, new life forms began to emerge, including the precursor of modern gymnosperms, known as progymnosperms, tree-form horsetails, towering tree-form club mosses, and seed ferns.

planet in lethal strength. The first plant life began to change all that. Ancient algae, like all green plants, created food for itself by photosynthesis, using sunlight, carbon dioxide, and water to create sugars to use as food *(page 26)*. A byproduct of this process is oxygen. Over hundreds of millions of years, oxygen created by algae in the oceans escaped into the atmosphere, where some of it was transformed by sunlight into ozone, forming a protective layer in the

Exactly when plants first made the transition to *terra firma* is not known, but fossil evidence shows that it began about 400 million years ago. Surviving in this foreign environment required major adaptations. Water was no longer freely available, but had to be extracted from the soil, so specialized tissues—roots—were developed to absorb it. In addition, a vascular system was needed for moving water from the roots to the top of the plants and bringing the food created by photosynthesis back down, while rigid tissue was required to hold up the plants in their search for more sunlight.

EARLY ADAPTATIONS

Cooksonia, the first known land plant, was about two inches (5 cm) high, with symmetrical branches. On the tip of its branches were spore-producing globules called sporangia, which generated tiny male and female spores about the size of fine dust particles. Spore-based reproduction relies on the wind or rain to bring the male and female spores together for fertilization and to place them in an appropriate environment in which to grow.

About five million years after *Cooksonia* took hold, another type of plant appeared. Also symmetrically branched, it produced spores along the sides of the branches rather than at the end. Although apparently minor, this change was a reproductive advantage because each plant produced more spores, resulting in a higher number of successful offspring.

In this same time era (called the Devonian period, which extended from about 395 million to about 345 million years ago), many new plant types developed, including trimerophytes, which had a main stem and lateral branches like modern trees rather than the earlier symmetrically forked pattern. Some trimerophytes developed woody tissue that added strength to the stem and increased their ability to move water upward, enabling them to grow taller. As the number of plants increased, competition for sunlight made height an advantage and the descendants of trimerophytes became the earliest form of trees.

THE FIRST FORESTS

The Earth of 350 million years ago looked very different from the planet of today. The land masses were still connected and were surrounded by shallow, relatively warm

Like the ancient plants that would one day spawn the first trees, giant kelp has no need for an elaborate root structure—water is everywhere. When plants invaded the land, however, they needed to develop a way to tap into water in their new home and they also evolved woody tissue that would allow them to stand upright.

13

seas. The climate was essentially unchanging year-round and generally warmer and more humid than at present. In this swampy landscape, the first forests thrived. Club mosses and horsetails grew to tree-like proportions of more than one hundred feet (30 m), herbaceous plants filled in the forest's middle canopy, and new forms developed, including ferns that grew up to twenty-five feet (8 m) tall. When these plants died, they fell into the swampy water, where they did not fully decompose due to lack of oxygen. Instead the partially decomposed plant material eventually turned into peat, which, after millions of years of compression from added layers of soil and plant material, became today's coal beds. The period from roughly 345 million to 280 million years ago is named the Carboniferous for this reason.

CLIMATIC CHANGE

At the end of the Carboniferous, Earth underwent a period of geological upheaval and climatic change that lasted millions of years. The woody giant club mosses and horsetails began to die out, leaving only the smaller, herbaceous versions that we know today. The drier, colder climate was less favorable to these plants, which prefer abundant water and have spores that need more humidity to keep from drying out.

In this climate, gymnosperms began to dominate. These trees, which had first appeared during the Carboniferous, flourished partly because of a new reproductive device they shared with the seed. The name gymnosperm comes from the Greek words for "naked seed" and refers to the fact that these trees bear their seeds exposed on structures similar to leaves. This offers an advantage

Ancient Reminders

The Petrified Forest of eastern Arizona, stone tree stumps found in New York and in Scotland, and other petrified forests found around the world have given scientists a fascinating way to study the structure of ancient trees. A particular set of circumstances is required to turn a living tree into a petrified one. If the tree is buried quickly by a layer of fine material such as volcanic ash, silt, or mud and if water penetrates into the cell cavities, carrying with it minerals and other solid materials that eventually turn to stone, a perfect cast of the tree's internal structure may be created. In the case of ancient trees from the araucarian forest of Argentina, some cones are so well preserved that single seeds are visible around the core of the cone.

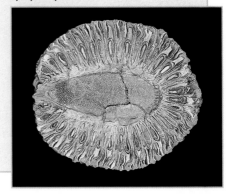

over spores: Seeds, by virtue of being covered with a skin, are resistant to drying out, and they have the possibility of dormancy—they can wait until conditions are right before germinating. Modern conifers such as firs, pines, and spruces are descended from these early gymnosperms, and several "living fossils" survive from this period. One, the ginkgo (*Ginkgo biloba*), or maidenhair tree, distinguishable by its fan-shaped leaves, is widely planted as an ornamental. And the cycads (*Cycadophyta*), with their squat trunks and tufts of palmlike leaves, still grow wild in the tropics and subtropics.

THE MODERN FOREST

Gymnosperms dominated the arboreal world for more than a hundred million years, but eventually they were relegated to less favorable habitats: windswept mountainsides, sandy soils, and the colder, northern regions, where they still dominate the boreal forests of Eurasia and North America. The territories they gave up were taken by the flowering angiosperms, the name of which means "covered seed."

These plants, which first appeared in the fossil record about 120 million years ago, have many reproductive advantages over gymnosperms. The hard coating of angiosperms' seeds provides protection. In some species, their flowers attract carriers—birds, bees, beetles, and other insects—that bring male pollen and female ovules together, while gymnosperms rely

A relic of early seed-producing trees and little changed in more than 200 million years, the monkey-puzzle tree (Araucaria araucana) of Chile is part of the family Araucariaceae. A perfectly preserved cone of a tree that was included in these ancient conifers is shown on the page opposite.

exclusively on the wind. In addition, most gymnosperms produce cones whether or not they have been pollinated, whereas most angiosperms will produce a fruit only after pollination and fertilization.

With all of these advantages, along with improved vascular systems and deciduous leaves, it is no wonder that these plants eventually flooded the world with a hundred thousand species—more than one hundred times the number of gymnosperms species that still exist on Earth.

HOW TREES WORK

*It's easy to forget, when looking at the graceful beauty of a tree,
what a remarkably complex organism it is—a marvel of
engineering that challenges anything humans have ever constructed.*

Regardless of their shape or size, all trees are essentially living chemical-processing factories. They draw moisture and nutrients from the soil through their roots and transport these raw materials up to the foliage through the vascular tissue of the sapwood. The foliage, in the form of leaves, needles, or scales, serves as an array of solar receptors that capture the energy of sunlight. With this energy, the nutrients and water provided by the roots and carbon dioxide extracted from the air are broken down and recombined in a process called photosynthesis *(page 26)*. The carbohydrates resulting from this process consist of plant sugars, which are then transported down the inner bark and used as food by the cells of the part of the tree that is actually growing, a microscopically thin layer called the cambium.

Modern science has probed photosynthesis thoroughly, identifying the essential catalyst as a unique substance called chlorophyll. Science has also documented how the

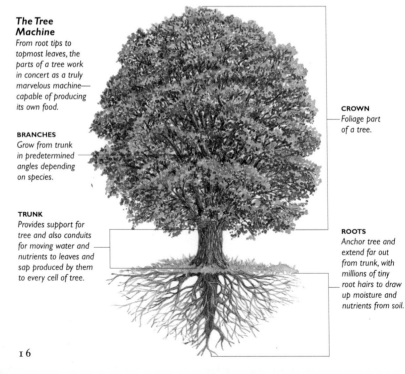

The Tree Machine
From root tips to topmost leaves, the parts of a tree work in concert as a truly marvelous machine—capable of producing its own food.

BRANCHES
Grow from trunk in predetermined angles depending on species.

TRUNK
Provides support for tree and also conduits for moving water and nutrients to leaves and sap produced by them to every cell of tree.

CROWN
Foliage part of a tree.

ROOTS
Anchor tree and extend far out from trunk, with millions of tiny root hairs to draw up moisture and nutrients from soil.

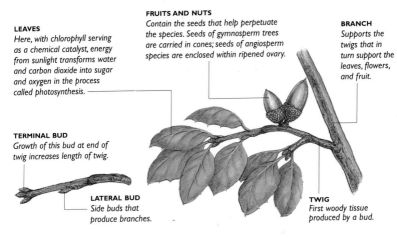

LEAVES
Here, with chlorophyll serving as a chemical catalyst, energy from sunlight transforms water and carbon dioxide into sugar and oxygen in the process called photosynthesis.

FRUITS AND NUTS
Contain the seeds that help perpetuate the species. Seeds of gymnosperm trees are carried in cones; seeds of angiosperm species are enclosed within ripened ovary.

BRANCH
Supports the twigs that in turn support the leaves, flowers, and fruit.

TERMINAL BUD
Growth of this bud at end of twig increases length of twig.

LATERAL BUD
Side buds that produce branches.

TWIG
First woody tissue produced by a bud.

various organs of a tree—roots, vascular tissue, leaves, and bark—work to promote the process. But despite this detailed knowledge, photosynthesis has never been duplicated in a laboratory—a surprising fact, considering its importance for all life on Earth, providing the plant and ultimately the animal kingdoms with the food they need to survive.

Trees also play an important role in the transpiration of ground water, releasing it as moisture into the atmosphere. Although trees retain a certain amount of moisture as sap, what is retained represents only a small fraction of the water that they must drag up from the soil to keep the process of photosynthesis going. This is because the upward flow of water acts as a conveyor of other trace elements,

> *". . . it is a pleasant thing to see a tree grow . . . Without a love of trees, I doubt if there be any art."*
>
> — RICHARD JEFFERIES (1848-1887)

such as iron, copper, nitrogen, and magnesium. In fact, without magnesium, the chlorophyll molecule could not be constructed and without chlorophyll, photosynthesis would not be possible.

Perhaps most amazing of all is how this organic chemical factory manages to maintain and coordinate the process with neither a brain nor a central nervous system. Still, the tree is not without its own means of guidance and control. A key part of the system appears to be the terminal buds *(above)*. Although science still lacks a firm grasp of exactly how they work, the buds control the tree's machinery with hormones. Under their direction, the tree leafs, flowers, grows, sets fruit, repairs itself, and, with the help of pollination, perpetuates its kind.

Pollination

While a great variety of broad-leaved trees, from cherry trees (*Prunus*) to magnolias (*Magnoliaceae*), are prized for their colorful, fragrant blooms, the fact is that all trees produce some type of flower. The conifer version, called strobili, or cones, are small and lack colorful petals. Once pollinated, the female versions of these "flowers" grow into the familiar cones we see on pines (*Pinus*) and their relatives. Some flowering trees, such as willow (*Salix*), birch (*Betula*), and oak (*Quercus*), also bear non-showy flowers called catkins, named for their resemblance to miniature cat tails.

Whatever form they take, all flowers are involved in the same basic function: pollination, the production and transfer of microscopic pollen grains among flowers. The first step in tree fertilization and sexual reproduction, pollination sets in motion a chain reaction leading to the production of seeds and fruits. Observed under a microscope, pollen grains from different plant and tree species differ greatly in shape, size, and color. Each grain contains genetic information needed by the egg cell, or ovum, to produce an embryo. Some trees are self-pollinating, or are capable of self-pollination if pollen from other trees isn't available. Many other trees depend strictly on cross-pollination, or pollen from other trees. This is true of many important fruit trees.

An eastern hemlock (Tsuga canadensis) emits a cloud of pollen into the wind.

DISTRIBUTING THE POLLEN

One of the disadvantages of being literally rooted to the ground is that trees have to rely on outside forces to distribute pollen—and, later on, seeds as well *(page 20)*—thereby ensuring survival of the species. Many trees depend on the wind. In these cases, huge quantities of pollen are released from flowers to improve the odds that a single microscopic pollen grain will hit its equally tiny target. A catkin flower on a birch tree can discharge more than five million pollen grains, and one tree may bear several thousand

Tough Customers
The outer shell of a pollen grain is so tough and durable that it can resist decay for thousands of years. By studying ancient pollen retrieved from successive layers of a peat bog, paleobotanists can re-create the history of the ancient flora in the region.

catkins. In springtime, puddles on pine-forest floors are often covered with a thick film of yellow pollen from surrounding trees.

Relying on the wind for pollen dispersal has both advantages and disadvantages. In its favor, wind can carry pollen great distances (up to several thousand miles). At the same time, it is an undirected, haphazard means of distribution, and since pollen is very high in oils and proteins, the great quantities needed represent a huge expenditure of a tree's energy.

As trees and flowering plants evolved, insects and other creatures, such as birds and bats, began playing a crucial role in more accurate and efficient pollen dispersal. Attracted to a

flower's scent, colors, nectar, or the pollen itself, these creatures flit among flowers and unwittingly distribute sticky pollen grains that rub off their body.

Sometimes elaborate and exclusive symbiotic relationships develop and a tree species and pollen carrier become totally dependent on each other. Fig wasps are a fascinating example of this phenomenon. Each of the nearly one thousand species of fig trees (*Ficus*) in existence is pollinated by a different species of fig wasp. Fig wasps grow up inside figs and the fig tree's tiny, unusual flowers grow in this same cavity. Once the wasps have matured and mated, the males dig a hole through the flesh of the fig. Using this hole as an exit, the females fly away to lay their eggs inside different figs; meanwhile, carrying clinging pollen, the wingless males never leave the fig during their life.

Mammals are important agents of pollen dispersal. Here, pollen from a banana tree coats the fur of a greater short-nosed fruit bat, which will carry it to another tree, helping to pollinate it.

The Seeds of Life

After fertilization of the ovum occurs, all trees develop seeds, marvelous packages that contain an embryo with food to sustain it during the infant tree's first growth. Tree seeds vary remarkably in size. European silver birch (*Betula pendula*) seeds are so tiny that it takes 400,000 to make up two pounds (1 kg), while a single coconut (*Cocos*) can weigh forty-five pounds (20 kg) *(page 22)*. A towering 350-foot (110-m) coast redwood (*Sequoia sempervirens*)—the world's largest living thing—casts its future generations to the wind in tiny seeds smaller than a fingernail.

Some birds, such as the cedar waxwing above, excrete seeds from the fruits they eat. Others rely on regurgitation. The quetzal of Central America, for example, is able to swallow an avocado, remove the fruit in its crop, and then expel the stone.

The two main groups of trees produce seeds in very different ways. Gymnosperms generate seeds without a surrounding fruit. The seeds develop inside female cones, which open their scales when they mature and dry out, releasing their contents. The seeds of angiosperms, on the other hand, develop inside a flower's ovary. The ovary of maple (*Acer*), ash (*Fraxinus*), oak (*Quercus*), apple (*Malus*), and a host of other angiosperms are transformed into fruit, a vehicle designed to increase the seed's chances of germination and subsequent growth. As with conifers, the embryo of angiosperms is surrounded by a reserve of starch and protein to provide food for the infant tree and a shell, or seed coat. With angiosperms, the fruit may also include a fleshy outer covering.

Whether seeds are "naked" or encased in fruit, they are designed to respond to the trees' reproductive dilemma: How to disperse their offspring widely so that all won't develop in the parents' shade? Various adaptations have developed to accomplish wide dispersal. Many seeds have outgrowths of seed coats in the form of thin, papery extensions that allow long-distance gliding. Elms (*Ulmus*), many conifers, and ash are among the trees with wind-transported seeds. Willows (*Salix*), poplars (*Populus*), and birch (*Betula*) have feathery catkins, fluffy seed carriers that can be blown far and wide by strong winds. Maples have developed samaras—twin arrangements of winged seeds that spin like helicopter rotors to keep them aloft as long as possible. Other trees float their seeds on water rather than on wind. The tiny seeds of alders (*Alnus*) contain a droplet of oil that helps them to float.

SWEET SEDUCTION

Seeds packaged in fruits are dispersed by animals attracted to the nutritious flesh. Many fruits contain seeds that are protected by coats tough enough to pass through digestive tracts unharmed. The seeds then germinate wherever the dropping falls. Other fruits have edible flesh encasing poisonous or very large seeds that will be discarded. In most biomes, birds are important seed distributors. Trees that "want" their fruit to be eaten signal to birds by having their fruit become brighter colored when ripe. In the tropics,

monkeys are also great seed dispersers, homing in on bright fruits with their color vision. In more temperate areas, many seductive fruits, such as nuts and acorns, are transported by rodents, especially squirrels. Instead of protecting the seeds with tough or poisonous seed coats, these trees produce fruits in huge numbers to ensure there is more than enough to serve as food. (A single oak tree, for example, may produce fifty thousand acorns a year.) This way, rodents unwittingly plant trees throughout their range when they bury nuts here and there, but return to eat only some of them while forgetting the others.

THE BIRTH OF A TREE

When provided with air and suitable moisture and temperature, the seed may absorb water and germinate. Then again, it may not.

The squirrel's less than perfect memory is often the genesis of a new tree. The animal often doesn't return to retrieve what it has so carefully hoarded, thereby leaving new seeds planted firmly in the ground.

The seeds of the coco-de-mer (Lodoicea maldivica), found in the Seychelles Islands, are the largest of any plant, weighing up to forty-five pounds (20 kg). The two-lobed design of the shell has earned it the nickname "the double coconut."

In the tropics, quick germination is fine. In colder zones, however, germination after fruit production could lead to a frozen infant tree. As a built-in safeguard, seeds adapted to frostier regions have to undergo a period of cold weather followed by warmer temperatures before germination can take place. Some of the same seeds are also prompted to germinate by the unusually high heat of a forest fire. For example, the jack pine (*Pinus banksiana*) and lodgepole pine (*P. contorta*) release their seeds en masse after a fire, when a cleared forest creates excellent germination and growth conditions *(page 42)*.

Germination in the springtime is often triggered by light, especially in deciduous forests, which have not yet sprung their canopy of leaves. Once germination has been initiated, the nascent plant begins to grow, fed by digestion of the surrounding food. The first part of the plant to break out is the root, which responds to the

Sea-going Seeds

For long-distance seed dispersal, no tree can beat the coconut palm (*Cocos nucifera*), which sends forth its seeds by water from its seashore home. Coconuts protect seeds inside their hard, buoyant shell. They may float for months before washing up on shore—sometimes thousands of miles from where they started—before finally germinating.

Vegetative Propagation

With all the perils of seed transportation and germination, it's not surprising that some trees propagate vegetatively. Broken branches of willows (*Salix*), for example, may root and begin to grow if they are transported to a suitable, wet environment. Poplars (*Populus*) send up suckers from their roots to become young trees. While bypassing the risky fruit and germination stage seems a great move, vegetative reproduction has two big disadvantages. Good dispersal of young trees is unlikely and the offspring are identical to the parent, eliminating the possibility of improving the stock through the exchange of genes. Willows and poplars counteract this problem by also producing seeds for reproduction.

force of gravity and probes downward into the soil. Then, the stem shoots up above ground. This first growth is fueled by special seed leaves, called cotyledons, that develop into the first green photosynthetic part of the plant. Flowering plants have either one or two of these seed leaves, while gymnosperms may have more than ten of them. Then, when true leaves form, the seed leaves wither and fall off, the last of the parents' resources used up. The infant tree is now on its own.

The first few months of a tree's life are more hazardous than the decades or centuries that may follow. Competition for its needs is severe, and the vast majority of young plants wither and die shortly after they start growing. Because pushing its stem up above ground may be hampered by twigs or leaves, the initial push must be strong; the germinating and growing tree sends up its stem while the base is still embedded in the seed. Even fairly heavy objects can soon be pushed aside and it is not unusual to see a young tree that germinates in a crack in a sidewalk or road actually lifting up sections of broken pavement in its quest for survival.

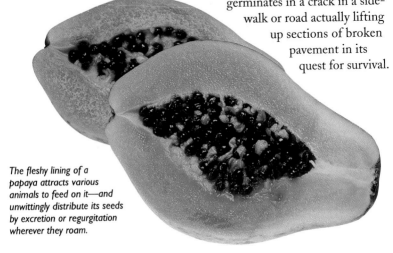

The fleshy lining of a papaya attracts various animals to feed on it—and unwittingly distribute its seeds by excretion or regurgitation wherever they roam.

Putting Down Roots

Roots are not just the anchor that holds a tree in place through wind and storms; they also provide a tree with the water—up to nine hundred gallons (3,400 l) per summer day for a single birch, for example—

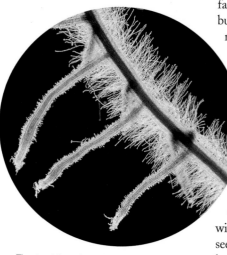

The tiny, delicate hairs that grow at right angles to the root absorb moisture and nutrients from the soil. Each hair, actually a single cell, attaches itself to particles of soil, extracting the life-giving moisture and nutrients from them.

and the nutrients it needs to survive. Anyone who has ever dug up a tree is familiar with the most visible part of a root system, the twisted, soil-colored organs that snake their way through the ground. But the heart of the network—the part that absorbs the nutrients and water and allows a tree to live and grow—consists of millions of tiny, white hairs that sprout near the root tip, invisible to the naked eye.

RUDIMENTARY ROOTS

In most trees, the radicle, or primary root, develops into a long, branching taproot that helps anchor the tree. Since most nutrients are located within five feet (1.5 m) of the surface, taproots are usually not deep, but they have been known to burrow more than one hundred feet (30 m) in moisture-poor, sandy soil.

Shallow, crisscrossing lateral roots branch off the main roots. The length of these roots depends on the species, type of soil, and surrounding environment, but they usually extend far beyond the outermost branches of the tree.

Large-seeded trees such as oaks usually have a long taproot with small lateral roots, while small-seeded trees such as birches typically have similar-sized, horizontally growing radicles and lateral roots. In all, the root network of a large tree may number millions of roots.

The end of each root burrows with a corkscrew motion called circumnutation, following the path of least resistance. If an obstacle is encountered, a root tip will invariably veer around it. The tips are protected by a continually renewing layer of cells called the root cap.

Roots are pushed forward by about three pounds (1.5 kg) of force from the growing pressure of delicate white hairs poking out from behind each root tip. These microscopic hairs trap oxygen and

Strange Roots

In soils low in oxygen, trees can grow breathing roots, also known as pneumatophores, to provide them with the air that their anchor needs to survive. In the case of mangroves, roots grow up through the mudflats where these trees are often found and are exposed to the air during low tide. The baldcypress (*Taxodium distichum*), a denizen of freshwater swamps, also grows breathing roots, which push above the waterlogged ground in strange, nobbly projections as tall as three feet (1 m) *(right)*.

nutrients, and wrap around soil particles to absorb their water. Highly selective membranes in the hairs permit passage of some elements into the roots and limit that of others as needed, while allowing only a one-way flow of nutrients to prevent leakage back into the soil.

COOPERATION AND COMPETITION

Many roots grow intertwined with the thin threads of a fungus, mycorrhiza, a symbiotic relationship that forms a critical link between the roots and the soil. The fungus produces enzymes that break down organic matter, enabling the roots to better absorb nutrients from the soil around them. In return, the fungus receives carbohydrates from the host plant. Insects and animals also help. Worms aerate the soil, while rabbits and badgers drag nutrient-rich leaves underground. In return, their home deep beneath the trees is protected by the roots and kept relatively dry.

The crisscrossing network of a root system of a tree can spread for hundreds of square feet. The only portion of a root that actually lengthens, however, is the part just behind the protective cap at the tip. Roots grow as much as one inch (2.5 cm) a day during the height of the growing season.

2 5

The Workings of a Leaf

Small valvelike openings called stomata, which are usually located on the underside of a leaf, are clearly visible through a microscope. Stomata open and close according to weather conditions and the time of day, and control the exchange of gases between the leaf and the outside air.

Leaves vary tremendously in shape and size, from tiny needles to large, leathery broadleaves, and they are often the most distinctive and beautiful feature of a tree. Some leaves grow separately, while others feature several leaflets in a compound design. Leaves can have a lobed shape, such as the maple leaf, or they can be rounded, long, and thin or shaped like a tear drop. The edges of some leaves are smooth; those of others are jagged. The possibilities are almost endless and help serve as important clues in the identifying of a particular species of tree *(page 72)*.

NATURE'S FOOD FACTORIES

No matter what their shape, all leaves carry out photosynthesis. During this remarkable process, leaves utilize carbon dioxide from the air and energy from sunlight to create the carbohydrates that trees need to grow. Leaves not only act as food factories for a single tree or plant, but are also the first link in nature's food chain—the primal source of life on the planet. Once the sun's energy is chemically captured by a leaf and the leaf or some other part of the plant is eaten by a herbivore, the stored energy is released again. In turn, carnivores eat herbivores and so on up the chain.

The flat, broad surface of a leaf is called a blade. To allow maximum absorption of the sun's rays, the sap-carrying stalk, or petiole, angles the blade so that it presents its full surface to the sun *(box, page 28)*. Leaves are webbed with strong, thin veins that keep them stiff and flat and serve as a kind of plumbing system. One type of vessel carries water into the leaf from the branches and stems, while another transports newly created carbohydrates from the leaf to the rest of the tree. These veins branch out into smaller and smaller vessels until they reach microscopic size.

Despite being nearly paper thin, a leaf is a complex, highly specialized structure. Below its surface, or epidermis, a leaf contains two layers of tissue. Both layers are made of cells that contain chlorophyll, a pigment that gives leaves their characteristic green color and serves as the catalyst in photosynthesis. The tissue layer closest to the leaf's top surface—known as the palisade layer—is thin and densely packed with these photosynthetic cells; the lower layer is spongy and loosely packed, providing it with ample air spaces.

Air enters a leaf through tiny openings called stomata, which are usually located on the underside of the blade, and moves through the spongy layer of cells into smaller air spaces in the palisade layer. As sunlight hits the leaf

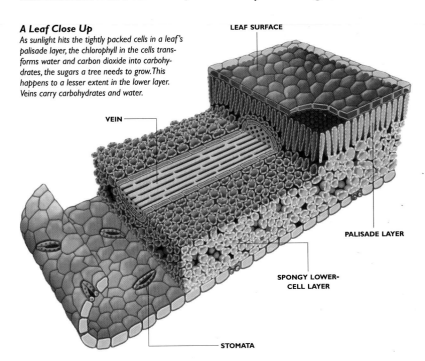

A Leaf Close Up

As sunlight hits the tightly packed cells in a leaf's palisade layer, the chlorophyll in the cells transforms water and carbon dioxide into carbohydrates, the sugars a tree needs to grow. This happens to a lesser extent in the lower layer. Veins carry carbohydrates and water.

LEAF SURFACE

VEIN

PALISADE LAYER

SPONGY LOWER-CELL LAYER

STOMATA

Bending to the Light

To capture as much energy as possible during photosynthesis, trees tilt their leaves to expose the full blade to sunlight. This is accomplished with hormones called auxins, just one of several types of tree hormones that regulate growth. Auxins move to any part of a growing stem that is hidden from the sun. The hormones cause the cells in those shaded areas to grow more quickly (becoming elongated) than cells on the well-lighted stem, which may in fact stop growing altogether. The push and pull between quick-growing and slow-growing cells results in stems that twist the leaf toward the sun. The scientific term for this phenomenon is called heliotropism.

surface, its energy is ensnared by chlorophyll and used to turn water and carbon dioxide into carbohydrates, releasing oxygen as a byproduct. The carbohydrates are then carried from the leaves to all parts of the tree. No simple explanation can do justice to this complicated photochemical process. Even chemists who devote their working lives to unraveling the mysteries of photosynthesis don't fully understand all the details.

The stomata not only take in air, but release it as well; and they allow water vapor to flow in and out of the leaf. Stomata (which is the Greek word for "mouths") function as valves and are controlled by two kidney-shaped guard cells on each side of the opening that deflate and swell up as needed. When they deflate, the cells collapse against each other to close the opening; as they swell up, they regain their kidney shape and a channel forms between them.

In hot, dry weather, stomata close to restrict water loss and prevent the leaves from drying out. However, this also reduces the absorption of carbon dioxide, slows down photosynthesis, and leads to slower tree growth. In cooler, more humid weather, stomata open wider so that more air can flow through. Stomata also open and close in response to light. Water loss is also reduced by the waxes or resins that cover and protect the leaf.

A Colorful Show

With the cool, dry days of autumn, deciduous forests in the temperate climates of North America put on a spectacular display as leaves turn from green to reds, yellows, and golds. This occurs because as the daylight hours decrease, chlorophyll production slows down and eventually stops, revealing yellow, gold, and orange pigments—called carotenoids—that were present in the leaf all summer but hidden by the chlorophyll. At the same time, another new group of pigments is produced in the leaf, which contribute the red, scarlet, and purple hues. These so-called anthocyanins are stimulated by sugars that remain trapped in the leaves.

SHEDDING AND BUDDING

The needles of most conifers and even evergreen hardwood trees are shed slowly over the year—or several years in the case of coniferous trees *(page 30)*—as they lose their resilience. Deciduous trees discard their leaves at the end of the growing season as daylight hours decline or the dry season begins. Although leaf buds are associated with spring, stems in fact develop buds the previous summer, where they remain hidden at the axil, the joint where a leaf meets the stem. The topmost bud on a given branch is called the terminal bud. It is often larger than other buds because it also contains a flower embryo. Growth of buds that form at the axil is controlled by hormones that diffuse from the terminal bud. If the terminal bud is damaged, shoots that grow from the axillary buds may extend quickly to take over the role of the terminal buds.

Buds develop into leaves very quickly, fed by sap from the roots and nutrients stored in wood tissue. They are usually pale green, and soft and delicate at first, although in some tree species, budding leaves are bronze-colored or reddish brown. Right from the start, or at least as soon as leaves turn green, the chlorophyll becomes active and photosynthesis begins.

Needles & Scales

While angiosperms have broad, sun-capturing leaves that usually fall off when cold weather approaches, gymnosperms, which feature flattened, scalelike leaves. Needles and scale-shaped leaves are covered with a thick, waxy cuticle to reduce moisture loss, which helps counteract the low humidity of winter days. The long and narrow shape of conifer needles reduces surface area exposed to air, further reducing moisture loss.

The needle-shaped leaves of conifers and their tough, waxy covering are perfect foils to the load of winter snow. In addition, the trees' branches slope downward so snow slides off instead of building up to branch-cracking weight.

Because of their waxy coverings, needles and scales are less efficient solar collectors—relative to the amount of energy required to produce them—than broad leaves. It is therefore not surprising that leaves on most conifers live for at least a few years to save the trees the taxing task of replacing them annually, as angiosperms do. For example, the needles of a red pine (*Pinus resinosa*) will die and drop off the tree after three years, while those of a balsam fir (*Abies balsamea*) can survive as long as seven years.

include conifers, have developed a much different type and shape of leaf. The most common coniferous leaf, borne by pines (*Pinus*), spruces (*Picea*), and many others, is long, narrow, and needle-shaped. The shape and the number of these needles per bundle are important clues for identifying a particular species *(page 72)*. Other conifers, such as white cedar (*Thuja occidentalis*),

The evergreen strategy of conifers, although energetically costly, has one great advantage. While broad-leaved trees shed their leaves well before extreme cold and then grow them back only when warmer weather has returned, conifers can photosynthesize whenever the temperature rises above fifty-two degrees Fahrenheit (11°C). High in mountains and in northern forests, the growing season may be just a few months long and this extra time to gain energy from the sun is critical. This enables gymnosperms to dominate the huge tracts of northern boreal forests.

Strangely, the best-adapted to cold of all conifers is not an evergreen. Several species of larch lose their clusters of needles in the fall and regrow them in the spring. This makes them deciduous coniferous trees. In fact, the most northerly of all conifers is the Siberian larch (*Larix sibirica*), growing to the tree line at seventy degrees latitude in Siberia, where even antifreeze-protected needles might still freeze in extreme cold. Larches also often form the tree line on high mountains. Although deciduous, larches hold their needles longer than most broad-leaved trees in the fall and regrow them earlier in the spring. This gives them a head start on broad-leaved trees at the same latitude. Their needles are light and short, requiring less energy to produce than the waxy leaves of most conifers. Three other conifers, baldcypress (*Taxodium distichum*), golden larch (*Pseudolarix amabilis*), and dawn redwood (*Metasequoia glyptostroboides*), have adopted a deciduous strategy.

Hot Stuff
Unlike the foliage of broad-leaved trees, which are full of sap and therefore difficult to ignite, the needles of evergreen conifers are loaded with resins that make them particularly flammable—a fact well known to fire fighters who battle explosive fires that involve these trees.

Some gymnosperms have even developed broad leaves. The ginkgo (*Ginkgo biloba*), an ancient tree that dates back to the time of the dinosaurs, has fan-shaped leaves that are completely unlike classic conifer scales or needles. The genus *Podocarpus*, another coniferous tree, has also developed broad, ovate, and flat leaves.

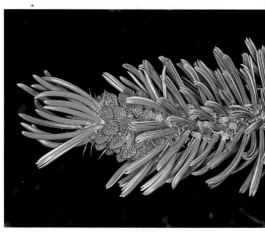

Cold that would freeze a broad-leaved tree's foliage is no problem for conifers, since their needles are protected with a natural liquid antifreeze.

How Trees Grow

In contrast to what happens with animal life, the tissue of a tree doesn't disappear when it dies. With the exception of the foliage, which may be seasonally replaced, and the slow flaking off of the outer bark, virtually all of the biomass a tree produces through many decades or centuries of life remains visible. In a mature tree, the living tissue accounts for a very small portion of this biomass, perhaps 1 percent or less. In fact, the only continuously living tissue in a tree that contributes to growth consists of a microscopically thin film of cells between the sapwood and the inner bark called the cambium layer, which encases the entire tree from the tip of the branches down the trunk and out along the roots. There is also a second cambium

layer, called the bark cambium, on the outside of the inner bark. It, too, is continuously living, but unlike the primary cambium, this layer does not contribute to tree growth. Instead, its sole purpose is to create the outer, corklike bark needed to both protect and insulate the tree.

The cambium cells in the primary cambium layer are unique in that they produce daughter cells both on the inside and to the outside as they divide. The cells on the inside become woody tissue called xylem, while those to the outside take the form of inner bark, or phloem. These two layers of newly formed tissue function much like a divided highway. The xylem immediately to the inside of the cambium layer is called the sapwood, and it is

A Slice of Life

The trunk of a tree connects the roots with the leaves in a circulatory system as elaborate as a medieval cathedral. Water and nutrients are drawn up from the roots through the xylem, while the sugary sap produced by the leaves through photosynthesis returns through the phloem. Between the two layers lies the cambium—the one-cell-thick layer where cells divide and create new tissue, enabling the tree to growth in girth.

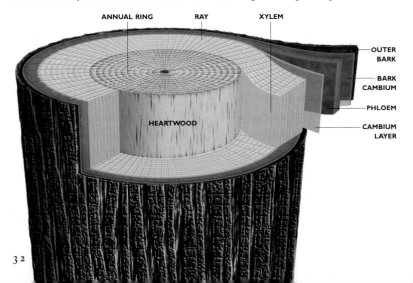

made up of tubelike cells that conduct sap—nutrient-rich water—from the roots up to the leaves. The phloem, on the other hand, brings carbohydrates down from the leaves to keep the cambium layer supplied with what it needs for continued growth.

THE HEART OF A TREE

While the sapwood and inner bark represent the primary highway for conveying sap both up and down, the tree also utilizes horizontal bands of conductive tissue called rays, which radiate out from the pith of the tree like the spokes of a wheel. Since the interior wood cells of a tree are dead, they require no sustaining nutrients themselves, but they are nonetheless useful as a storage place for nutrients and other compounds called wood extractives, typically gums and resins. The ability to convey these extractives into the interior cells via the rays is extremely important to the long-term health of the tree. The antiseptic qualities of the extractives help to prevent decay, maintaining the structural integrity of the tree. Also, the extractives tend to harden and polymerize into pigments over time, making the heartwood more rigid and usually darker in color.

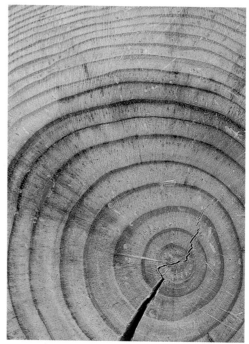

The dead inner core of a tree is known as the heartwood. It is typically darker in color than the surrounding sapwood and is prized by cabinetmakers.

As the cambium cells continue to divide and produce woody tissue, the tree grows in girth, but this growth does not progress with absolute uniformity in all species. Those species that have adapted to the finite growing season of a temperate climate seem to explode with vitality as they leaf out in the spring. The vascular woody cells produced at this time tend to be large in diameter, allowing them to conduct a maximum flow of sap. As the growing season progresses toward late summer, the cambium layer begins to produce stronger, heavier-walled cells, giving the woody tissue a laminate quality that provides maximum strength with minimum weight. It is this alternating pattern of growth that produces the so-called "annual rings" seen on the end grain of a tree stump. However, the more correct term for this feature of wood anatomy is "growth increment," since many tropical species exhibit a similar pattern based on wet and dry seasons that are not always precisely annual.

While the cambium layer functions as the engine of growth, it is capable of expanding the tree only in terms of girth. Extension of the main stem and branches occurs at the lead, or terminal, buds. Despite their small size in relation to the great mass of a mature tree, these buds function like operational control centers. While the complex chemistry involved in this process is perhaps the least understood aspect of plant physiology, it is known that the buds produce a vital growth hormone called auxin *(page 28)*, which congregates on the dark side of a stem or branch, with a resulting increased rate in cell growth on that side that forces the stem to bend in the opposite direction, toward the light. Another regulating hormone, called kinetin, also affects the process and seems to be responsible for telling the cambium cells what shape and kind of tissue they should become.

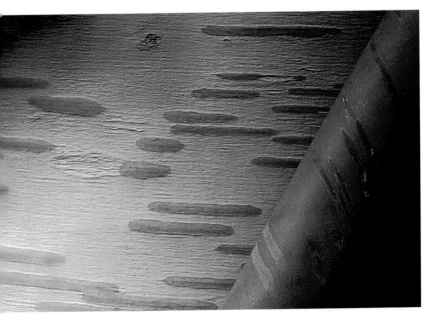

Bark on a tree can range from the paper thin covering of a birch tree (above) to the two-foot (60-cm) -thick protective cover that helps shield sequoias from forest fires.

Water Transporters

The plants that first colonized the land had rhizoids—rootlike projections—that enabled them to tap moisture in the soil. The moisture was then transported by vascular tissues made up initially of elongated tube-like cells called tracheids. The tracheids connected to each other by means of valvelike structures called pits, which allowed moisture to pass from cell to cell in a continuous stream all the way from the roots to the topmost leaves. Gymnosperms,

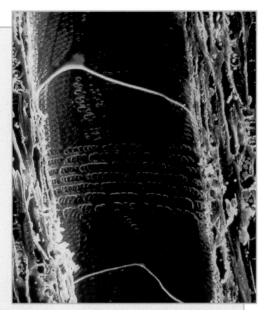

such as pines (*Pinus*) and other conifers, still employ this simple vascular structure. However, angiosperms, such as oaks (*Quercus*) and maples (*Acer*) have enhanced the efficiency of their vascular tissue by developing large-diameter tubes with walls that are made up of many cells *(above)*. While angiosperms possess tracheid-like cells, they have been relegated primarily to a support role as fiber cells. Still, there are advantages to the tracheid structure. Freezing or drought can create bubbles of gas that may block up large vessels, whereas the interconnectedness of tracheids allows small sections to be blocked without impeding the overall flow of moisture. This is one of the reasons that gymnosperms are more successful than angiosperms in cold or dry climates.

Regardless of which anatomical structure is employed, the truly ingenious part of the process of transporting sap is how trees have solved the problem of moving it vertically against the force of gravity. For some species, such as the coast redwood (*Sequoia sempervirens*), the vertical lift may exceed 350 feet (110 m). This herculean task is made possible by the cohesion property of water. Just as raindrops bead up on the hood of a well-waxed car, water molecules have a very strong affinity for each other. When confined within the narrow tubes of vascular tissue, this cohesive force is strong enough to hold a vertical column of water as much as a mile high without being overcome by gravity. Yet the only force necessary to pull this column upward is supplied by simple evaporation, the minutely small tug created as the leaves transpire moisture. Perhaps what is most amazing is that under ideal conditions, this flow may move along at a speed of as much as 150 feet (46 m) per hour. The tree retains only about 1 percent of the water for its metabolic needs, evaporating off the other 99 percent just to keep the system delivering other crucial trace elements dissolved in the sap.

Branching Off

While some trees, such as the pines (*Pinus*), tend to set their branches in whorls at spaced intervals up the trunk, giving them a noticeable and appealing symmetry, the configuration of most trees looks like a confused jumble of opportunistic growth. But this sort of seemingly haphazard branching is by no means random. In fact, there is a very precise order to how each species of tree sets its branches and even to how the leaves are positioned on the twigs.

The vascular tissue in trees does not track straight up from the roots, through the trunk, and then out along the branches. Instead, it progresses in a corkscrewlike spiral, making numerous revolutions along the way between root tip and the terminal bud at the end of each twig. This configuration of growth provides a very important survival benefit: Should the part of the trunk be damaged on the side facing the predominant source of light, the rotation of the vascular tissue allows the tree to branch off in that direction at some point later along the trunk.

Just as this spiral growth pattern facilitates the primary purpose of the trunk and the branches in providing a platform for arraying the leaves toward sunlight, it also plays a role in leaf placement. Because the purpose of the leaves is to capture sunlight, it is important that they don't shade each other. To accomplish this, the leaves bud out at various points along the spiral so that the next leaf further out on the twig grows out in a different direction.

A quick glance at a tree may not reveal the perfectly symmetrical growth pattern of its branches because some may be missing—damaged when they were twigs or simply having failed to develop. But the traces of these branches would still be visible at a predetermined angle from the previous ones on the trunk.

Corkscrewing growth
Both the leaves and the branches of a tree occur at a predetermined number of degrees of spiral rotation from the previous ones. This is made possible by the corkscrewing growth pattern of the tree's vascular tissue. Among the trees that rely on a 180-degree rotation (above) are elm (Ulmus) and basswood (Tilia).

DIFFERENT ANGLES

While all trees employ this basic spiral strategy for both branch and leaf placement, there are many variations on the theme and the exact spacing around the spiral differs from species to species. For example, some trees, such as maple (*Acer*), ash (*Fraxinus*), and dogwood (*Cornus*), set their leaves in pairs, one leaf opposite the other at the same point along the twig. The next pair will then be placed further out on the twig after exactly ninety degrees of spiral rotation. Most species, however, employ what is called alternate placement. With this format, only one bud is set at a given point along the spiral, but the intervals of rotation for setting each subsequent bud differ widely, depending on the species. In the case of elm (*Ulmus*), the next leaf bud will appear after 180 degrees of rotation, placing it both further out along the twig and on the opposite side. Beech (*Fagus*), on the other hand, divides a complete circuit of 360 degrees into thirds, placing buds at intervals of 120 degrees of rotation. Still others employ the more complex spacing of 144 degrees. In this case, two complete spirals are made around the twig before a bud is placed so that it is in perfect alignment with a previous bud. Determining whether a tree has alternate and opposite placements of leaves is one step in identifying a particular species *(page 72)*.

Complicating the situation still further, some species do not employ the same spiral direction for the entire life of the tree. For example, a sapling may begin its growth using a right-handed spiral and then, after several growing seasons, switch to a left-handed spiral, only to switch back again at a later time. This switching back and forth creates what is known as interlocked grain and occurs in many species, including elm and bigleaf mahogany (*Swietenia macrophylla*).

Tree Diseases & Pests

Trees can live hundreds or even thousands of years. Throughout their lifetime, they face attack from multitudes of pests and diseases—from the tiny spores of fungi and the gnawing teeth of deer and moose to the voracious appetites of various insects and their larvae. Why do some trees succumb while others survive?

SOLID PROTECTION

A solid layer of bark is a tree's best protection against disease. Fungal spores, bacteria, and viruses have a tough time getting through it to damage the living tissue underneath. But there are avenues of attack. Fallen limbs, grazing deer, or fire damage may leave wounds in the bark, open areas that allow intruders to gain a foothold. Some fungi, such as *Ganoderma applanatum*, can enter a tree through these wounds and grow in the inner wood. Although the fungi does not visibly damage the tree, which continues to grow as usual, it creates a core of decay in the trunk.

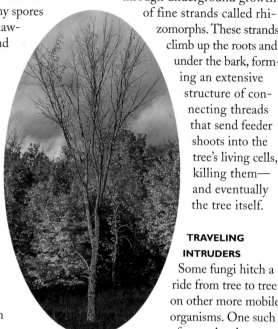

This American elm (Ulmus americana) *has been decimated by the Dutch elm disease. The fungus can kill a tree quickly, often in only one season.*

Other fungi, such as the honey fungus (*Armillaria mellea*), spread from one infected tree to another through underground growth of fine strands called rhizomorphs. These strands climb up the roots and under the bark, forming an extensive structure of connecting threads that send feeder shoots into the tree's living cells, killing them—and eventually the tree itself.

TRAVELING INTRUDERS

Some fungi hitch a ride from tree to tree on other more mobile organisms. One such fungus has been destroying elm trees (*Ulmus*) in Europe and North America since the 1920s with the help of the elm bark beetle. Dutch elm disease is caused by the fungus *Ophiostoma uln* or its close relative *O. novoulni*, which attacks the vascular system of elm trees. The fungus is carried from tree to tree by the elm bark beetle (*Physocnemum brevilineum*), which lays its eggs under the dead bark of infested trees. When the beetles emerge in the spring, they fly to other trees to eat the young bark of new growth shoots, carrying the fungus spores on their body. As they eat, they damage the bark and the underlying xylem layer, which allows the spores access to the inner parts of the tree.

The first sign of infection is usually wilted leaves on some branches in the crown of the tree. As the disease progresses, more leaves will turn yellow and then die, and eventually the entire tree will succumb.

Preventing infection is more successful than attempting to save an infected tree. Fungicide can be injected into healthy trees every couple of years as a preventive measure and may occasionally save an infected tree if less than 10 percent of the crown is damaged. Generally, preventive measures focus on controlling the elm bark beetle. Pruning dead limbs from healthy trees reduces potential egg-laying sites. Coating the lower six feet (2 m) of healthy trees with insecticide in the fall controls adult beetles, which spend the winter near the base of the trunk of healthy trees.

FOREIGN INVADERS

In a natural forest environment, trees live side by side with a host of pests and diseases, any one of which could kill them under the right circumstances. Fortunately, the right circumstances are not common. Healthy trees can often survive a fungal infection, perhaps losing only a limb or two. Insect pests are generally kept under control by birds and other predators. But when an insect or other pest is introduced into that environment from outside, havoc reigns since no natural methods exist to control it. One such devastating invader is the gypsy moth (*Lymantria dispar*).

The silkworm larva represents an intractable foe to mulberry trees (Morus), the leaves of which it consumes with an insatiable appetite. But there is one positive side effect. What the larva does not absorb from the leaf is then excreted as silk.

Trees as Pests

Sometimes, trees themselves can be a serious threat to other vegetation—and animals as well. When introduced into a new environment, they compete with native species, often upsetting the delicate balance of an ecosystem. The tamarisk (*Tamarix*), or saltcedar *(right)*, for example, introduced into the United States from Europe in the 1800s, is now considered a pest in the West. Tamarisks grow along riverbanks, soaking up water resources, crowding out native tree species such as cottonwoods (*Populus*), and altering the environment for other species of plants and animals. River habitats dominated by tamarisks tend to have reduced or less diversified populations of fauna than other habitats in the same areas. Reclaiming these habitats involves removing the tamarisks and replanting native species—an expensive and time-consuming task.

Introduced into Massachusetts in the late 1860s as a potential source of silk, the gypsy moth has been a major pest in North America ever since. A native of Europe and Asia, with no natural predators in North America, it spread rapidly; and as early as 1890, local and federal governments were attempting to eradicate it, with little success. The larvae eat the foliage of many plant species, but oak (*Quercus*) and aspen (*Populus*) are most often selected. A single infestation of moths can strip all the leaves from a tree. Such defoliation is a major stress, retarding a tree's growth and leaving it more vulnerable to disease. If complete defoliation occurs several years in a row, especially in combination with other stresses such as disease or drought, the tree may die.

The entire northeastern part of the United States is now infested, and new populations appear annually beyond the current range in spite of vigilant efforts to contain the gypsy moths. It seems inevitable that the range of the devastating insect will continue to expand.

Fighting Back

Rooted to the ground, trees can't run from threats—but that doesn't mean they're defenseless. Many trees, such as the African acacia (*Acacia senegal*), have thorns to discourage animals from eating their leaves. The acacia can even inject bitter alkaloids into its leaves; and at the same time, it emits ethylene gas to warn other acacias of the presence of a threat so that they inject their leaves with alkaloids, too.

Of course, these methods aren't foolproof; some leaves still get eaten, but enough remain to give the tree a fighting chance against competing vegetation. Some Central American species of acacia don't have the ability to make their leaves poisonous. Instead, they have developed an ingenious defense system with the help of colonies of stinging ants. Each swollen thorn acacia (*A. collinsii*) has its own colony of ants, which hollow out the acacia's enlarged thorns to make themselves a home *(below)*. The ants defend the tree against insects and mammals that would eat its leaves, and they cut away competing vegetation that threatens to steal its place in the sun. In return, the tree provides the ants with food—nectar from special glands at the base of each leaf stalk and protein-lipids from structures on its leaf tips.

Slowing the spread may be possible, however. One technique that has been tried is introducing biological agents known to kill the gypsy moth, such as certain small mammals, viruses, and fungi, into the infested areas. Aerial spraying of insecticides is also used in an effort to control outbreak populations discovered in previously uninfested areas.

Baptism by Fire

The public perception of forest fires is that they are a disaster with no redeeming qualities. Many scientists question that view, however, believing that these conflagrations may actually perform useful functions.

A forest fire is a capricious instrument of destruction. Firebrands, burning branches, and other debris are blown high into the air. Some may land a mile or more from the main fire, igniting new spot fires that cut their own swath through the forest, sparing some areas and leaving others torched in their path. Fighting such fires is difficult, dangerous, and often futile. In many cases, they are extinguished only with the assistance of nature—rain, snow, or a shift in the winds. Increasingly, forest managers and fire fighters are coming to understand that stopping such fires is, in fact, undesirable from nature's point of view.

As long as there have been forests, there have been forest fires. Growth rings from felled trees show scars from regular conflagrations. Some giant sequoias (*Sequoiadendron giganteum*) in thousand-year-old groves in California show evidence of fire roughly four times per century. In other areas, fires may occur more frequently, every five to twenty-five years. In fact, the health of the forest as a whole may depend on periodic fires. In temperate zones, the rate of decay is much slower than the rate of growth. Fire speeds up the process of decomposition, releasing nutrients stored in dead but undecayed vegetation for use in new growth. The extensive fires in Yellowstone National Park in 1988 are expected to result in the long run in a great increase of new plant species. In the first growing season after a fire, twice as many plant species may appear in the burned areas as were there before. This accelerated diversity persists for many years and is reflected in increased fauna as well.

Even larger fires can be beneficial. After the Yellowstone fires, the forest showed a characteristic "mosaic" pattern of burned areas: Some areas were spared, some charred. This pattern results in pockets of young regrowth within a mature forest, creating a diversity of habitats for wildlife species. In addition, plant species already in the forest may be able to expand their range. For example, new aspen (*Populus*) seedlings were found in burned areas shortly after the fires in Yellowstone.

Frequent small surface fires, which burn off low-growing ground cover and surface litter, appear to reduce the chances of larger, more destructive fires. Many insect pests live in this litter, so surface fires may help keep these populations in check.

Six years after the devastating 1988 fire in Yellowstone National Park, lodgepole pines (Pinus contorta) had already sprung up from the blackened soil, the result of special cones that open only when heated.

INCREASING THEIR CHANCES OF SURVIVAL

Many trees have developed strategies for survival. Thick bark protects mature pines (*Pinus*) and oaks (*Quercus*); the leaves of others, such as maples (*Acer*) and beeches (*Fagus*), are particularly fire-resistant. Some species even use fires to promote their development. Lodgepole pines (*P. contorta*) have two types of cones. One type releases its seeds at maturity. A second type opens only under intense heat. These seeds can wait, dormant, for years. After a fire, lodgepole pine seedlings often dominate the new growth *(above)*, even when mature lodgepole pines were only a small percentage of the previous forest. Jack pines (*P. banksiana*) also have heat-sensitive seeds and regenerate quickly after a fire.

A CL215 water bomber can drop up to twelve hundred gallons (4,500 l) of water in a few seconds on a forest fire. The planes are particularly effective in terrain too treacherous or remote for fire fighters.

HUMANS & TREES

From earliest times, humankind has relied on trees for many essentials, from fuel for fires to foods, medicines, and the makings of shelter.

Trees have played a central role at every stage of human history, providing fruits, nuts, and other foods, supplying fuel for heating and cooking, and offering a strong but easily shaped material that could be used for anything from weapons to a plow or a spinning wheel. Today trees remain a highly valuable resource. Still prized for fruit and lumber, trees offer much else besides—from bark extracts used in medicine to sap from which rubber is made. Unfortunately, human consumption of the world's resources put increasing demands on the environment, posing new challenges for how forests will be managed in the future.

The most popularly grown tree fruit, apples (Malus) have been cultivated for more than two thousand years.

STRENGTH IN LUMBER
Many bygone civilizations were even more dependent on trees than our own. The cedar (*Cedrus*) forests that once covered the hills of Lebanon were a hugely important natural resource for both the ancient Egyptians and the Romans. In addition to using durable cedar lumber to build ships,

houses, and temples and cedar resin for embalming the dead, the Egyptians employed the wood as rollers to move the stones that became the great pyramids. The Phoenicians, who lived in Lebanon, became rich exporting wood and wood products to the Egyptians. The first-known conservation legislation in history was enacted by Roman Emperor Hadrian, who ruled between A.D. 117 and 138. To ensure a supply of lumber for the Roman navy, he made a section of the mountains of Lebanon a forest reserve.

Made from the springy wood of the yew tree, the medieval English long bow signalled the end of the age of the mounted knight. In the battle of Agincourt in 1415, English soldiers equipped with their new weapon decimated their French opponents.

VALUABLE RENEWABLE RESOURCE

As humans developed techniques for smelting metals, wood—charcoal wood, in particular—became a critical resource as fuel for furnaces. With the rise of the Iron Age in the tenth century B.C., the new sharp axes spelled the end of many of the mixed oak (*Quercus*) forests that spread through much of Europe and Asia. Much later, in medieval times, all the forests remaining in Europe were claimed and carefully guarded by powerful men, such as lords, dukes, and bishops, who valued the woodlands not just for their various products, but also for the game animals that lived there.

The concept of wood as a renewable resource developed in the Middle Ages in the form of a technique called coppicing. This involved cutting down certain broadleaf trees so that the stumps sprouted shoots. Benefiting from the existing root system, the shoots grew very quickly and could be harvested in seven to twenty years, at which point new shoots would sprout again.

By the sixteenth century, forests were increasingly seen as national assets, particularly with the growing importance of shipbuilding. Wars were fought over lumber supplies, and various countries were plundered for their trees. When

"O if we but knew what we do
When we delve or hew—
Hack and rack the growing green!
Since country is so tender
To touch, her being so slender."

— GERARD MANLEY HOPKINS
Binsey Poplars

From the planks of sailing ships such as the ones used by Columbus (above) to the slats of dog sleds of Arctic travelers, wood has been a vital factor in human exploration.

Napoleon's armies cut off Britain's traditional lumber sources in the Baltic, the English developed new sources around the world, from Canada to India.

With the vast quantities of fuel needed to make iron in blast furnaces, a substitute for charcoal was badly needed by the eighteenth century. After the development of successful techniques for using coke, derived from coal, the Industrial Revolution gathered momentum and the demand for wood dropped slightly. Iron and steel also began replacing wood in major industrial sectors such as shipbuilding and bridge building. Still, lumber continued to play a key construction role in major nineteenth-century enterprises such as railroads and mines.

FOODS FROM TREES

Fruits have been an important source of food for foragers since the dawn of mankind. When meat or fish were scarce, nuts and seeds provided necessary protein and fat. These included coconuts and cashews in tropical regions and hazelnuts, walnuts, and beechnuts from temperate forests. All continue to be eaten in significant quantities today, although now they are typically cultivated. At one time, even acorns and hickory nuts were regularly eaten by certain North American Indian tribes, after being leached of their acrid and poisonous tannic acid. Acorns were a staple of the Pomo Indians of California, who made a kind of flour with them that they used in breads and soups. Acorns were eaten in Europe, but most often during times of famine.

With the rise of fruit cultivation, these formerly wild foods rose to a new level of economic and nutritional importance. Humans have been cultivating fruit for thousands of years. The date palm (*Phoenix dactylifera*), for example, has been cultivated for about five thousand years, and records from thirteenth century B.C. indicate that Rameses II of Egypt ordered apple trees to be planted in the Nile Delta—an ill-conceived idea since apples are a temperate fruit. The Greeks were cultivating many varieties of apples by the seventh century B.C., but the fruit was an expensive commodity. By Roman times, however, apple cultivation had become so extensive that the fruit was available to the average citizen.

IMPROVING NATURE'S BOUNTY

Immense time and effort has gone into adapting fruits to human needs and tastes. This has been accomplished by planting seeds from only those trees that produce the best fruit and by grafting two trees together or by coaxing cross-pollination in an effort to combine promising attributes of each *(page 52)*. Originally the apple was a small bitter fruit. Today more than a thousand varieties of apple are cultivated.

During the last hundred years or so, developments in food processing, storing, and distribution have all but eliminated dependence on local harvests. The twentieth century saw a huge increase in fruit exports around the world, as technologies developed for transporting fruit quickly and under conditions that keep it from spoiling. It also witnessed a vast and potentially catastrophic increase in the distribution and range expansion of many agricultural pests, such as the gypsy moth *(page 40)* and the citrus canker, which is presently devastating Florida limes.

Increasingly sophisticated genetic technology has also been used to develop fruit that stays fresh for longer periods and to increase fruit yield. This has left some consumers worried about food safety, while proponents of such technology envision an end to world hunger *(page 53)*.

Sweet Music

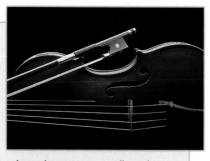

Wood was undoubtedly one of the first natural materials used to make musical instruments. Just as different trees have different characteristics, so, too, does the wood sawn from them. Sitka spruce (*Picea sitchensis*), for example, has one of the highest strength-to-weight ratios of any wood, making it ideal for the demanding role as the top, or soundboard, of a steel-stringed guitar. Brazilian rosewood (*Dalbergia nigra*) is the wood of choice for bow makers because of its resilience, while the toughness of ebony (*Diospyros ebenum*) makes it ideal for piano keys and bagpipe drones. Some instruments feature a variety of woods. Violins, for example, often use spruce (*Picea*) for the soundboard; maple (*Acer*) for the back; willow (*Salix*) internally for blocks and linings; and a dense hardwood such as ebony, rosewood (*Dalbergia*), or boxwood (*Buxus*) for the fittings.

From Log to Lumber

Before power saws and steam and gasoline engines, converting standing trees into lumber was grueling work. Today machines replace much of the

The chainsaw has been replaced in some forest operations in the United States by a machine called a feller-buncher, which can not only cut down a tree, but also trim its branches.

muscle power, but it still takes skilled people to carry out each step in the process. Undetected defects, damage during felling, improper bucking, and careless sawing can all lower a tree's value and plank output while raising mill and product costs.

TIMBER!

Fellers must consider a host of factors, such as site condition, wind direction, lean of the trunk, and dead branches—also known as widow makers—before cutting down a tree. First, they make a low undercut on the side where the tree will fall. A second cut with a chainsaw meets the undercut to remove a wedge about one-third of the tree's diameter. A back-cut is then made a few inches higher and almost as deep on the side opposite the wedge. The fall direction is controlled by a hinge of wood between these opposite cuts.

Once the tree has been felled, the limbs are removed, the larger ones slated for use as timber and pulpwood and the smaller ones burned or left to rot. The tree, which can range from the size of a small pole to a 180-ton mass two hundred feet (60 m) long and ten feet (3 m) in diameter, is skidded to a staging area, or landing, then cut into logs, or bucked. Trees too large for transport may be bucked at the felling site.

On steep hills, a cable supported by tall masts can be rigged in the air. Cables called chokers that dangle from the main cable are wrapped around the logs, which are hoisted into the air and reeled up the hill to the staging area.

Before cutting, the bucker scans the tree for signs of defect. These include bark bulges, concealing knots close to the surface, and wide, rotting branches—often a sign of decay within the trunk. In order to avoid defects, the bucker may decide to reduce the intended log length. For example, a sixteen-foot (5-m) -long hardwood log may be cut down to ten or twelve feet (3 or 4 m).

A tractorlike skidder truck hauls logs from the forest to a landing. The logs are then loaded with a hydraulic grapple hook, or log loader, onto timber trucks, large flatbedlike vehicles that can transport up to fifty tons. In countries with good river systems, such as Finland, logs can also be transported economically by water.

AT THE MILL

Sawmills are sometimes named for their saw types and the woods they process—a softwood band mill, for example. Large logs from softwood trees are usually cut by the larger band saws, which produce less waste. Sawmills with circular saws have a smaller capacity and are much less expensive to run than band sawmills. They are often used to cut smaller-diameter hardwoods.

Some logs are used as is, "in the round," for fencing and telephone poles. At the mill, the bark is stripped off with grinding cutterheads or blasted off with high-pressure hoses. Logs are then loaded onto a sliding cradle, or log carriage. Before the first board is cut, the sawyer must look for defects to maximize the board yield from each log. Larger mills have computers to help. In some cases, the sawyer can direct a laser beam

A sawyer at a sawmill in southern Vermont sharpens the blade on his four-foot (1.2-m) -diameter circular saw.

The Dawn of SmartWood

Wood is one of the world's few renewable and sustainable resources. But heavy demand has considerably reduced the size of forests and rendered many once-plentiful species rare—or even unavailable. Laws now forbid the export of freshly cut Brazilian rosewood (*Dalbergia nigra*), for example. Faced with the ban, cabinetmakers have begun looking for suitable alternatives. Guidance is offered by a program known as SmartWood. Set up by the international nonprofit organization Rainforest Alliance, SmartWood certifies forest products that come from well-managed, sustainable sources. To be awarded the SmartWood seal of approval, a provider has to satisfy various stringent, environmentally friendly guidelines. So far, nearly one hundred operations worldwide in boreal, temperate, and tropical forests have been certified as SmartWood providers, including growers of tropical hardwood trees such as bayo (*Aspidosperma cruentum*), chakte-kok (*Sickingia salvadorensis*), chontaquiro amarillo (*Diplotropis* spp.), and tornillo (*Cedrelinga cateniformis*).

down the log's length to help visualize cuts before they're made and control a mechanism to position the log on the cradle accordingly.

First, four outer slabs are cut, one from each face. After the log is squared, the next cut produces a board from the clearest, widest, most valuable plane, the "opening face," followed by boards from the remaining three faces. With small mills and small logs, the sawyer may cut successive boards from the opening face, opting for maximum-width boards rather than best grade. In either case, the remaining square core, the cant, is resawn into various sizes of lower-grade dimension lumber. The sawyer again determines optimum cutting strategy.

Boards are edged and trimmed to length according to wood type and intended final usage. The wood is sorted by size and species, after which the boards are graded. Those having the fewest defects—checks, knots, and lengthwise splits—are graded highest.

SEASONING THE WOOD

Water causes wood to swell with humidity and shrink in dry weather. The balsa tree (*Ochroma pyramidale*), for example, can absorb many times its weight in water. For cabinetry and anything but the roughest of carpentry work, wood must be seasoned, or dried to the moisture level of its intended environment. This minimizes future shrinkage and increases resistance to fungal decay and insects.

Boards can be either air- or kiln-dried. Air drying involves stacking boards outdoors (separated by strips of wood, called stickers, to allow air circulation) and covering them to protect the drying lumber from rain. This method has been replaced at most mills with kiln drying. In this process, wood is fed into a low-humidity, low-temperature chamber

A Cut Above

Many factors, such as the wood density, the fiber direction, and the concentration and kinds of resins and gums, can affect the quality of lumber. Even the way a board is sawn from a log can make a big difference both in the look of the wood and in how dimensionally stable it will be once it has been turned into a piece of furniture.

In plainsawn lumber, a log is cut into various-width planks with the growth rings roughly parallel to the face of the boards *(top right)*. Quartersawing involves cutting a log so that the growth rings are perpendicular to the face of the boards *(bottom right)*.

PLAINSAWN WOOD

QUARTERSAWN WOOD

The orientation of the growth rings plays a crucial role. If they are tangential to the board face, as they are in plainsawn lumber, when humidity levels rise, the wood can swell by as much as one inch (2.5 cm) over the three-foot (1-m) width of a tabletop. But if the growth rings are perpendicular, as in quartersawn lumber, there is very little swelling or shrinking. In addition, in some species, such as oak (*Quercus*) and sycamore (*Platanus*), the rays *(page 33)* are accented by quartersawing, producing attractive streaks on the board face. But all this comes at a price. Quartersawing wastes more wood than plainsawing, so cabinetmakers and others who buy these boards end up paying a much higher cost than for plainsawn lumber.

equipped with a fan and dehumidifier. As the moisture content of the boards falls, the temperature of the kiln is increased and the humidity further decreased. This process can reduce moisture levels to around 8 to 10 percent, compared to 15 to 20 percent for air-dried stock.

Veneers have been used in furniture making for four thousand years. The thin slices of wood are typically glued onto manufactured boards such as plywood or particleboard.

Tree Engineering

A shapely tree may be a natural beauty at its best, but these days it can also reflect the handiwork of a forest geneticist or a plant biologist. Increasingly, scientists are using biotechnology to increase trees' growth, their yield, and their resistance to pests and disease, while grafting continues to offer a less high-tech but effective means to create what nature would never itself provide.

GRAFTING

The goal of grafting is to join segments of two plants so they grow as one. The pro-

In an effort to improve the productivity of an orange tree, a branch is grafted onto parent stock.

cess allows fruit trees to mature early—most in less than two years—and to yield different fruit species on a single tree. With other trees, time for seed production can be reduced by half. In grafting, a scion cutting—a bud or a small branch—from a successful tree is attached by various methods to an established root stock or seedling to produce almost any type of fruit or nut tree. The root stock makes up the roots and sometimes the base of the trunk of the new tree. The scion will provide the rest.

Each part retains its identity in the newly grafted tree. When genetically improved seedlings are used for trees such as pines (*Pinus*), grafted trees produce stronger wood and superior seeds.

Grafting results are more successful when the cambium layer of the grafted portions are kept in close contact. In bud grafting, however, the cambium layers don't need to be aligned. Some grafted trees produce sucker shoots that sprout below the graft and must be removed to avoid crowding out the new growth.

BIOTECHNOLOGY AND TREES

With the inexorable demand for forest products, scientists are continually looking for ways to create trees with certain desirable qualities by the use of gene manipulation: transplanting genes of chosen qualities from other trees and organisms into the trees that they would like to acquire those traits. This so-called recombinant DNA technology can produce trees that withstand poor soil and low rainfall, while creating species that grow faster and wood products with fewer knots and stronger wood.

The research has prompted some controversy. Critics say that scientists lack enough understanding of how genes interact and that no one can foresee the future consequences of creating genetically modified organisms (GMOs). By combining genetic material from vastly different, barely related organisms, such as bacteria to apples or jellyfish to corn, genetic engineers risk opening up a Pandora's box, critics contend. Introducing a new, unrelated DNA sequence into a recipient organism may create unexpected effects on how that organism functions on the cellular level. Also, there is the risk of having genes escape from the target organism into closely related weed organisms, with possible devastating effects.

Squaring the Circle

Turning a round log into rectangular boards involves a lot of waste in the sawmill. One answer to this problem, according to plant geneticists, is to grow a square tree. This involves experimenting with the cambium cells of a tree and introducing genes that will allow the cells to grow square instead of round.

There are also some practical problems to overcome. Unlike crops such as tomatoes or canola, trees grow much more slowly and have genomes—the genetic instructions that direct life and growth—up to ten times bigger than those of humans. That makes locating a desired gene for transferring a time-consuming task. As one research biologist admits, "Trees are uncooperative experimental organisms."

A worker at a research station in Finland shields trees' female flowers from pollen carried freely by the wind. The flowers will then be sprayed by pollen from specific trees to produce progeny of known parentage.

Trees as Art

It is often said that you can't improve on nature—that the beauty of a tree, for example, represents perfection. But for centuries, gardeners with an artistic eye have looked on the natural beauty of a tree not as an end in itself, but as an inspiration. In every environment that supports both trees and people, trees are selectively planted and pruned to define the landscape in visually pleasurable ways. Tall trees line city streets, while carefully trimmed hedges create privacy for suburban houses. But while such plantings are functional as well as esthetically satisfying, certain specialized tree-sculpting techniques emphasize artistry above all.

THINKING SMALL: THE ART OF BONSAI

It is not clear when the Japanese art of bonsai originated. However, a depiction of these miniature trees on a scroll dated 1309 indicates that this highly spiritual gardening practice was well established by the dawn of the fourteenth century. A bonsai artist painstakingly prunes the roots and branches of a bonsai tree over the course of many years. This is done both to greatly restrict growth and to achieve a desired appearance. Most of these trees are roughly triangular in shape, although precise symmetry is frowned on. The look of a tree's trunk and branches are emphasized over the appearance of the foliage.

The biggest challenge is coaxing the trunk to grow to a sufficient thickness. If it remains too thin, the proportions of the tree are considered unappealing. The end result is intended to give the impression of a proud old tree in the wild enduring against the forces of nature. The tree species that lend themselves best to these techniques include junipers (*Juniperus*), azaleas (*Rhododendron*), pines (*Pinus*), and maples (*Acer*).

LOST IN THE GARDEN: HEDGE MAZES

The history of life-size mazes dates back to the ancient Greeks, who created perplexing pathways bordered by stones or mounds of soil. The use

Bonsai trees can live many hundreds of years and old trees with impressive pedigrees may fetch very high prices. In 1999 a six-hundred-year-old Japanese yew, once owned by Japanese royalty, sold at auction for $80,000.

Experienced maze-goers use various tricks to solve mazes such as this one at Hampton Court in England. For example, by keeping one hand on the side of the hedge and following it wherever it goes, in and out of every dead end, the maze explorer will eventually find the center.

of shrubbery to create mazes began many centuries later in Great Britain, where hedge mazes became popular features in the gardens of the country's stately homes.

From higher ground, the elaborate layout and precisely trimmed shrubs of a hedge maze create an eye-catching motif. Up close, these living labyrinths are intended as a source of entertainment—and sometimes frustration. From a more esoteric, religious perspective (the Church of England early on incorporated maze designs into its art), the winding paths of a maze symbolize the difficult route to salvation and the many twists and turns caused by sin.

There are two basic types of hedge mazes. One consists of a single, very indirect path leading to the center. With no false turns or dead ends, these unicursal mazes, as they are called, are intended as attractive curiosities. A second type of maze, the puzzle maze, is equally beautiful from a distance, but also carefully designed to confuse those who take up the challenge of trying to make their way to the center. In fact, it is not unusual for first-time visitors at a large hedge maze to spend hours taking one false turn after another before solving it. In the eighteenth century, the designers of Great Britain's most challenging mazes became well known and sought after for their skills.

Beyond Fruit & Lumber

The value of trees extends far beyond the fruit that we eat and the lumber we build with. Trees provide paper for books, the compound that tans leather, and some of the world's most popular beverages. They also furnish the stuffing for mattresses and many of the spices for our food. One tree product makes chewing

the spirits, maketh the heart lightsome." Botanists trace coffee's origin to Abyssinia and the name coffee may originate from the mountainous province of Kaffa, where coffee trees (*Coffea*) grow wild. Coffee trees have now been planted worldwide and the "cherries" are picked to produce the beans for roasting.

The sap from sugar maple trees (Acer saccharum) *has traditionally been gathered in metal buckets and then poured into large storage tanks drawn through the woods by a horse.*

gum chewy, another serves us the cork for our wine bottles, and still another protects buildings from earthquake damage.

OF BEVERAGES, SPICES, AND OTHER TREATS

Perhaps the most ubiquitous use of trees is as familiar as the morning cup of coffee. An early English advertisement trumpeted that the drink "helpeth digestion, quickeneth

A close runner-up for most popular beverage is tea. Commonly a shrub, the tea plant (*Camellia sinensis*) can attain treelike stature, growing wild in Southeast Asia. The Chinese were among the first to discover its merits; tea became a favorite drink of mandarins and emperors and choice varieties were literally worth their weight in gold. Introduced in Europe in the sixteenth century, the drink became immensely popular and whole fleets of ships were built to bring tea from the Orient. Spices, too, generated an ever-growing stream of shipping traffic between Asia and Europe. Cinnamon, cloves, and nutmeg were some of the precious spices derived from trees.

In the sixteenth century, the world came to know of another taste delight from trees after Spanish explorers of Mexico noticed the Aztec fondness for chocolate. Since then, the cacao tree (*Theobroma cacao*) has been planted in many lands. The six-to nine-inch (15- to 23-cm) pods are picked from the tree and five to ten seeds are extracted from the pulp-filled interiors to produce chocolate.

From native North Americans came another treat. In late winter or early spring, when snow is melting in the forests of northeastern North America, many maple trees (*Acer*) are the subject of a curious harvest. Holes are drilled into the trees' sapwood, releasing pressure built up within, and sap drips out into buckets or a network of plastic tubing. Collected and boiled in evaporators, sap undergoes an increase in its sugar content from 2 percent to 67 percent. The aptly named sugar maple (*A. saccharum*) is by far the main producer of maple syrup, but other species, such as black (*A. nigrum*), silver (*A. saccharinum*) and red maples (*A. rubrum*) can also be tapped.

FROM CORKS TO COATS

Bark from the cork oak (*Quercus suber*) has long been recognized as a unique and useful product. No other material, synthetic or natural, combines its qualities: It is lightweight, rot- and fire-resistant, able to compress and expand, impermeable, soft, and buoyant. Cork is used for floats, flooring tiles, gaskets, clothing, coasters, and, of course, wine corks. Cork oak plantations cover more than twelve million acres (5,000,000 ha) in several Mediterranean countries. Every ten to eighteen years, a cork oak has its bark stripped off, cut into slabs, and processed for use.

Trees also play a role in even the clothing we wear. For thousands of years, leather has been produced by

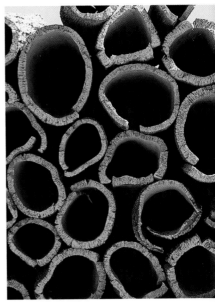

A cork oak (Quercus suber) *can produce cork for up to two hundred years.*

soaking animal skins in extracts of tannin. Tannins are chemicals found in bark and also in the wood, leaves, roots, and seeds of some trees. Leading sources of tanbark include the eastern hemlock (*Tsuga canadensis*) of North America, and the black wattle (*Acacia mearnsii*), introduced from Australia to form plantations in South Africa.

Diagonal notches in a rubbertree (Hevea brasiliensis) allow the milky juice of living cells—latex—to ooze out. The cut is made into the inner bark, but not into the cambium layer.

RESINS, GUMS, AND RUBBER

In many trees, rays that run like spokes toward the center of the tree trunk *(page 33)* carry resins, gums, and other compounds. Resins tapped from pines (*Pinus*) in Europe and the southern United States are distilled to produce paint-thinning turpentine. Pine resin also contains rosin, a substance that is used in printing inks. It can also be applied to violin bows to create more friction on the strings. Resins from other trees supply ingredients for various processed foods, medicines, and cosmetics.

Frankincense and myrrh, carried by two of the three biblical wise men as gifts to the baby Jesus, are resins tapped from trees. At one time, these sweet-smelling resins commanded lofty prices.

Probably the most-tasted of all tree products comes from the African acacia (*Acacia senegal*), a native of northeast Africa and Arabia. Nomadic tribes make incisions in the bark, returning a few weeks later to collect the oozing gum. This so-called gum Arabic was used as the adhesive of choice for stamps and envelopes. Although synthetics have replaced it in those applications, the sticky substance still has many uses—in the lithographic printing process; for the manufacture of smudge-proof watercolor paints; as a surgical adhesive to graft together severed nerves; and as a candy glaze.

Trees also supply natural rubber, which is produced from a latex that drips from wounds cut into the bark of the rubbertree (*Hevea brasiliensis*). In 1870 an English botanist smuggled a few infant rubbertrees out of their native Brazil. These trees, eventually planted in Southeast Asia, formed the beginning of huge plantations, and countries such as Thailand, Indonesia, and Malaysia currently dominate the natural rubber market. While synthetic rubber is now widely produced, the durability and flexibility of natural rubber continues to make it a sought-after commodity. Natural rubber was used to produce pneumatic subway tires in Mexico City, Montreal, and Paris, while some buildings are protected from earthquake shocks with natural-rubber insulators.

Central America's sapodilla tree (*Manilkara zapota*) provides another useful gum called chicle. Chicle supplies the chewiness in chewing gum, including the brand fittingly known as Chiclets.

NATURAL FIBERS, TOO

The natural fibers of trees have yielded a vast range of products. Fibers taken from leaf stems of the palm tree (*Calamus*) make excellent natural brushes and brooms. Ten thousand tons of brush-making fibers are still harvested from palms each year

and distributed throughout the world. Ropes, fishing nets, cloth, and matting are other natural tree-fiber products, while kapok fiber is still widely used as a stuffing for life jackets, cushions, and mattresses, as well as for insulation against heat and sound. The lightweight material, almost impervious to water, comes from the pods of the tropical kapoktree (*Ceiba pentandra*).

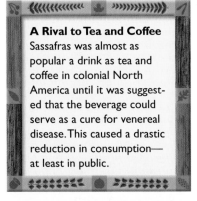

A Rival to Tea and Coffee
Sassafras was almost as popular a drink as tea and coffee in colonial North America until it was suggested that the beverage could serve as a cure for venereal disease. This caused a drastic reduction in consumption— at least in public.

Tea trees (Camellia sinensis) *can grow up to thirty feet (9 m) high, but in plantations such as this one in Sri Lanka they are pruned to a low shrub.*

The Medicine Tree

Every human culture has found in trees a kind of natural medicine chest. Cherokee women used black cherry (*Prunus serotina*) bark to ease

The cinchona tree produces several alkaloids, including quinine. The substance has been used to treat malaria since the seventeenth century.

labor pain. Ancient Greeks used cypress (*Cupressus*) cones steeped in wine to treat dysentery, asthma, and coughs. Arabians in the ninth century used the pods and leaves of the senna tree (*Senna alexandrina*) as a laxative. The examples are almost endless. Just how these treatments and countless others were developed is not known, but must have involved a mixture of trial

and error, luck, and observation of the animal world. According to legend, an Abyssinian goat-herder in the tenth century found his animals particularly frisky after they had eaten bright red beans from a certain tree and began experimenting with the beans himself. While it is impossible to say whether such an event really triggered the coffee craze that began during this period, it is certain that similar observations and experiments must have initiated the therapeutic uses of plants and trees.

Medically, the New World's most important tree is perhaps the cinchona (*Cinchona*), the bark of which provides quinine. Spanish conquistadors took the so-called fever-bark tree back to the Old World after 1600. Until then, Europe and Africa had no cure for malaria, a disease so lethal it had killed an estimated two million people annually for more than a thousand years. In 1944 wartime experiments led to a synthetic version. But the cinchona tree retains its usefulness because some new Asian strains of the malaria parasite appear resistant to synthetic quinine, but not to the natural substance.

For millennia, several willow (*Salix*) species have been used around the world to relieve joint pain and control fever. The bark from young branches of this riverbank tree is used fresh or dried; leaves are soaked. The active ingredient, first isolated in 1838, is the forerunner of acetylsalicylic acid which, as aspirin, is the most widely used medicine today.

The evergreen neem tree (*Azadirachta indica*) of India and Sri Lanka is a living drug-store. Its bitter, astringent bark can be applied to hemorrhoids; its leaves are steeped to treat intestinal worms or peptic ulcers; juice from its leaves is spread on ulcers, wounds, boils, and eczema; its twigs are used to clean the teeth. The strongly anti-fungal oil from its seeds is used to treat leprosy and is said to prevent lice, while the seeds are thought to be spermicidal.

According to some doctors, extract from the ginkgo tree can improve cognitive function in dementia patients.

The gingko (*Ginkgo biloba*), one of the world's most ancient trees, has been in the Chinese herbal repertoire for centuries, but western medicine only recently confirmed its efficacy in improving cerebral circulation and aiding memory and concentration. Gingko also appears to have potential as an anti-inflammatory, an anti-asthmatic, an anti-spasmodic, and an anti-allergenic.

Many of the drugs and medicines sold at modern pharmacies contain the same active ingredients as those in healing trees and plants. However, in most of the world, western-made pharmaceuticals are prohibitively expensive and plant-based drugs remain the norm. Meanwhile, in the west a renewed interest in plant- and tree-based medicines has been growing for several decades as modern science continues to find value in ancient treatments and researchers investigate the forests of the world for undis-covered remedies. Among the trees currently being studied are Australia's Moreton Bay chestnut (*Castanospermum aus-trale*) and the Japanese white pine (*Pinus parviflora*). Both are seen as offering potential treatments for people suffering from immune deficiency. Taxol, medication derived from the Pacific yew tree (*Taxus brevifolia*), is now being used to treat a variety of cancers.

Take Your Medicine
Oliver Cromwell, seventeenth-century soldier and ruler of Great Britain, refused to take quinine when he became ill in 1658, believing cinchona bark to be part of a papal conspiracy. It wasn't a wise decision. Cromwell ended up dying of malaria.

Interpreting Trees

The Library of Tree-Ring Research at the University of Arizona in Tucson contains several hundred thousand samples that have been used in research ranging from anthropology to forest ecology.

As school children learn in science class, the number of rings on a tree trunk usually corresponds to a tree's age. But tree rings reveal far more than when a particular tree sprouted from the ground. In fact, the study of tree rings, a field known as dendrochronology, has made valuable contributions to many branches of science, from climatology and ecology to history and archeology.

Tree rings are layers of wood cells produced by a tree over the course of a year. The contrast in appearance between the cells that grow at the end of one growing season and at the beginning of the next creates the ringed effect. Dendrochronology studies how weather conditions and other influences affect these rings. Favorable weather conditions lead to increased cell growth. This in turn results in a wider tree ring than would form if conditions had been poor. In other words, trees are living records of past weather conditions. Tree rings can also exhibit the effects of forest fires and plagues of insects.

Because a given tree species may respond to environmental conditions in a unique way, researchers can refine their information by studying more than one species at a time. The growth rings of some species may reflect nothing more than overall changes in annual rainfall, while in other species the rings are sensitive to changes in rainfall late in the summer. Thus, scientists may be able to determine, for example, not only whether summer in a particular region 821 years ago was rainy, but whether the month of August was particularly rainy that year. To establish how various trees respond to the same conditions, researchers study living trees with a set of devices called dendrometers. The findings are verified by replicating the data with multiple trees and are then analyzed using a variety of computer programs.

Considering that some trees live more than forty-five hundred years, much can be learned from a single specimen. Fortunately, it is not necessary to cut down a tree to study its rings. Instead, a special coring device is used to drill out a small sample of trunk tissue. However, researchers are not limited to studying live or recently felled trees. Dry climates preserve the remnants of dead trees reasonably well and fossils exist of wood thousands of years old. One way to date a long-dead tree is to compare its outer rings to the inner rings of an old living tree. If a corresponding pattern of rings is identified, it becomes possible to carry dating farther back into the past. Tree-ring chronologies that stretch back nine thousand years have been established for bristlecone pines (*Pinus longaeva*). Even longer chronologies now exist for European oaks (*Quercus*) and pines (*Pinus*).

In the 1920s A.E. Douglass, a professor at the University of Arizona and a pioneer of dendrochronology, led an expedition to an ancient settlement in New Mexico. By identifying ring chronologies in the timbers used in construction, Douglass proved that the village was built eight hundred years before the arrival of Columbus. Since then, information learned from trees has been used to date everything from volcanic eruptions to long-ago droughts. Dendrochronology has also served to fine-tune the results from radiocarbon dating, the technique that allows archeologists to determine the age of organic materials by measuring the amount of the isotope carbon 14 that they contain.

The study of past weather patterns revealed in tree rings is key to making more accurate predictions of future weather trends.

Trees in Trouble

Humanity has played a major role in altering both the condition and the composition of almost every biome on Earth. What is perhaps most alarming about this trend is the scope and speed of its progression.

The old-growth forests and virgin prairie that once dominated the temperate zone are now so depleted that vestigial remains of these biomes are increasingly becoming guarded national treasures in the form of national parks and monuments. The timeline over which this devastation has occurred in Europe and North America can be traced back several thousand years.

Establishment of forest reserves under the Roman Emperor Hadrian indicates that the process of deforestation around the Mediterranean was well underway in classical times. The primarily deciduous forests north of the Alps were essentially still intact at the time of the fall of the Roman Empire in the fifth century A.D., but by the dawn of the Age of Discovery a millennium later, the scarcity of timber for shipbuilding altered the military strategies of European nations as they vied for access to this strategic commodity elsewhere in the world.

Trees and their roots are the glue that hold soil together. Badly designed and poorly maintained logging roads can create erosion that wreaks havoc on the landscape.

In North America of the early seventeenth century, a vast and virtually undisturbed forest existed between the Atlantic coast and the Mississippi River. But by the end of the nineteenth century, the deciduous forests of the Midwest had been cleared, primarily to free the land for agriculture. Meanwhile, the coniferous forests of the Great Lakes had been logged and the lumber industry was already shifting its attention to the forests of the Pacific Northwest.

A TALE OF TWO BIOMES

Only two of the world's major forest regions, the predominantly angiosperm rain forests of the tropics and the coniferous boreal forests of Eurasia and North America, entered the twentieth century relatively unaltered by human activity. Two hundred years ago, tropical forests covered almost 20 percent of Earth's land surface. Even by the end of World War II, approximately 80 percent of tropical forests were essentially unexploited. But as Third World nations struggled to industrialize and also to feed their burgeoning populations, more than half of this once vast resource was eradicated in a mere five decades.

Of the approximately sixty thousand square miles (155,000 sq km) of tropical forest lost annually, more than two-thirds is either cut for fuel wood or simply cleared and burned to open the land for crops and pasture. And while the boreal forests of the northern hemisphere have fared better, they are now under increasing pressure to meet the world's needs for construction timber and also paper pulp and fiber for other industrial products.

Despite their great differences, boreal forests and tropical rain forests share an essential vulnerability: Both biomes are extremely fragile and difficult to manage. In the case of boreal forests, the growing season is so short that once trees are harvested, more than a century may pass before they fully regenerate. Rain forests, on the other hand, cannot be clear-cut without causing catastrophic leaching and erosion of the soil. Even selective cutting leads to the collapse of diversity within a rain forest and leaves it little more than an impoverished plantation.

OVERPOPULATION'S THREAT

Scientists now warn that unless the growth in human population is quickly stemmed, virtually all of the world's terrestrial plant biomes will have been extensively altered by human exploitation well before the close of the twenty-first century. The most alarming forecasts suggest that human activity is already altering the global ecosystem.

The ever-increasing use of coal and oil for power generation, heating, and transportation has led to both localized deforestation due to acid rain and a measurable increase in the proportion of carbon dioxide in the atmosphere. Elevated levels of carbon dioxide cause the planet to retain more heat—the so-called greenhouse effect, which could have serious, negative implications for humanity. An accelerated melting of the polar ice caps would flood many of the major coastal population centers. However, as the very term greenhouse suggests, higher carbon dioxide in the atmosphere and warmer global mean

Weakened by the effects of acid rain, parts of a forest in North Carolina near the Blue Ridge Parkway succumb to an infestation of woolly aphids.

This image, taken by a Landsat satellite, shows extensive deforestation of the tropical rain forest in part of the Amazon basin in Brazil. The dark green of the natural forest contrasts with the pale green areas—agricultural land—in the center. A network of roads dominates the right-hand lower quadrant of the photo. Loss of rain forest in South America is a major environmental concern. The forest is an important absorber of carbon dioxide and a moderator of climate.

temperatures might actually benefit plant life. Apparently, the global ecosystem has a powerful capacity for self-balancing, and forests and other plant biomes are renewable—if given the opportunity.

In recent decades in the United States, the annual increase in the forest biomass has actually exceeded the level of harvest. In other words, at current rates of consumption, the resource is still self-sustaining. But what these statistics mask is the continuing qualitative degradation of the world's forest biomes. Trees in managed forests are increasingly being harvested well before they reach full maturity, and technology contributes to this trend by providing new uses for forests, such as fiber, chips, and chemical extractives, that don't require trees of saw-log quality.

To further enhance productivity of trees, large areas of once diverse forests are being replaced by single-species plantations, seeded with genetically engineered cultivars or exotics that are imported from distant and often even quite dissimilar biomes. For example, radiata pine (*Pinus radiata*), a minor species of temperate zone yellow pine that was once found only in the Monterey area of coastal California, is now a major reforestation species in Australia and several other places in the southern hemisphere, while numerous species of high-value tropical timbers, such as teak (*Tectona grandis*) from Southeast Asia, have become important plantation species in Latin America and Africa.

In many instances, the genetic manipulation and translocation of tree species has proven very successful in terms of economic rewards. But there have been some catastrophic consequences, such as the decimation of the American chestnut (*Castanea dentata*). Once one of North America's most important hardwood timbers, it proved defenseless to a virus brought in on oriental chestnut cultivars imported as arboretum stock a century ago.

MANAGING THE RESOURCES

As the human population continues to grow, it seems inevitable that the world's forests will have to become more intensely managed to maximize the productivity of this resource. There is reason for optimism that this can be done in terms of increasing yields, much in the same way that it has already been accomplished in agriculture, but there are serious tradeoffs. The propagation of certain tree species by the exclusion of others to meet currently-known human needs simply mortgages the future. The primary risk is the loss of diversity, and this is especially true in the world's remaining rain forests, which host perhaps 90 percent of the world's terrestrial species. Even seemingly minor disruption in these intricate biomes cascades through the ecological interrelationships of species—both plant and animal—leading to a diminished gene pool and even to possible mass extinction in both kingdoms.

As science expands its understanding of genetic engineering, a reduction in the available gene pool would have serious repercussions, limiting the horizon for advancements in agriculture and many other fields of endeavor, including medical science. While an increasing proportion of drugs are now produced synthetically, historically the vast majority of these drugs were first discovered as naturally occurring compounds, most often of plant origin. At the present time, less than 2 percent of the world's 250,000 or more species of plants have been thoroughly researched for their pharmacological properties. To destroy diversity before its full potential has been explored seems both wasteful and foolish, to say the least.

Clear-cutting—removing all trees rather than selected ones from an area—allows more rapid replanting of the forest in a single-species plantation (above). But in areas such as untouched rain forests, clear-cutting results in a large loss of biodiversity. Logging in these forests has also been criticized for altering the circulation of air in the lower canopy, leading to a higher evaporation rate and lower moisture content in the forest biomass—a major contributor to the severity and increased size of forest fires.

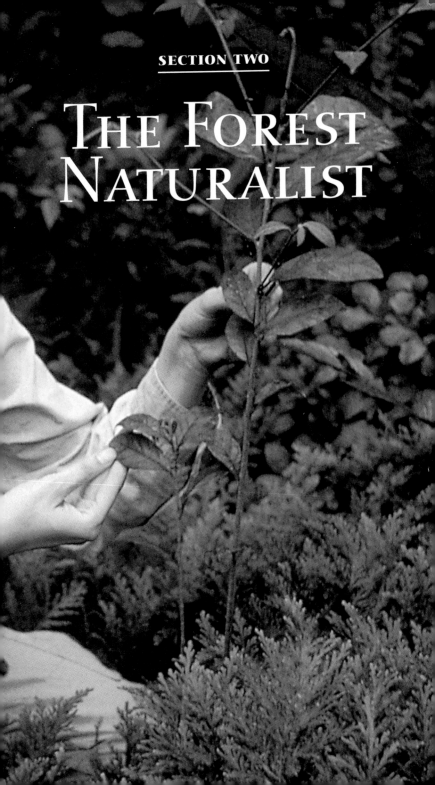

THE FOREST NATURALIST

IDENTIFYING TREES

The best way to learn about trees is to head outdoors with a guidebook in hand. By examining trees closely and knowing what to look for, you will discover remarkable variety and a wealth of fascinating details.

The tools of an amateur field naturalist include a camera, thick paper and a graphite art stick or crayon, a notebook, a guidebook, a long tape measure, a pocket knife, sample bags, and binoculars.

Whether you live in the city, country, or suburbs, the chances are good that you don't have to go far to study trees. While nothing beats a walk through a mixed forest for getting a look at a cross-section of tree species, you can also learn a lot in parks—and even in your own backyard. A few basic items of equipment will be invaluable in your explorations.

FIELD GUIDES

A field guide to trees is indispensable for the budding tree watcher. The identification guide in this book provides a solid foundation to get you started, with information on how to go about identifying a species, but you may want a more comprehensive source. Smaller bookstores usually offer at least one or two field guides and larger stores and Internet booksellers

> *"The admiral says that he never beheld so fair a thing: trees all along the river, beautiful and green, and different from ours, with flowers and fruits each according to their kind . . ."*
>
> — CHRISTOPHER COLUMBUS
> (1451-1506)

typically boast a wide selection. Guidebooks may cover an entire continent, a single country, or part of a country. In the case of North America, for example, there are guides for trees that are found from northern Canada to southern Mexico and other books that split the continent in two, east and west.

Most guides are designed to be small enough to fit into a pocket or a day pack, but these may not be as complete as larger, heavier volumes.

OTHER EQUIPMENT

In addition to a field guide, the following items are also useful: binoculars so you can see identifying features such as cones, nuts, and leaves of tall trees; a sharp pocket knife to cut samples; a stick for measuring tree height *(box below)*; plastic bags to store samples; a camera to record bark and other features (a zoom lens can be a helpful accessory); and a notebook and a pencil. Finally, if you are heading into the woods during the spring, take along some insect repellent.

Measuring the Height of a Tree

The height of a tree is often a good clue for identifying a species and is one of the characteristics included in the tree profiles at the back of this book. You don't have to climb the tree to find out how tall it is. Instead, cut a stick the same length as your fully outstretched arm. Hold the stick vertically at arm's length. Walk to a spot where you can align the top and bottom of the stick with the top and bottom of the tree. The distance that now lies between you and the tree corresponds to the height of the tree. Mark the spot and measure the distance with a tape measure.

Playing Detective

Because trees, unlike birds and mammals, don't fly or run away, you have the happy advantage of being able to take your time observing a specimen, walking around it and considering it from all angles, looking for clues to unlock its identity.

You've probably already noticed some of the distinguishing characteristics of trees—the typically pyramidal shape of spruce trees (*Picea*), the lobes of an oak (*Quercus*) leaf, or the mottled bark of the sycamore (*Platanus*), for example. Learning to identify different species is largely a matter of homing in on details.

Each species of tree has its own combination of leaf and bark characteristics; type of flowers, fruits, or cones; and habit—the way the tree grows (whether the branches curve up or point down, for example).

When you're learning to identify a new tree, details of leaf characteristics are probably the most important. The first distinction, between conifers and broad-leaved trees, is usually easy: Conifers have "leaves" that are either needlelike or scalelike; broad-leaved trees, as their name suggests, have broader leaves, with a flat blade and a central midrib. Identifying specimens within these two categories involves some detective work.

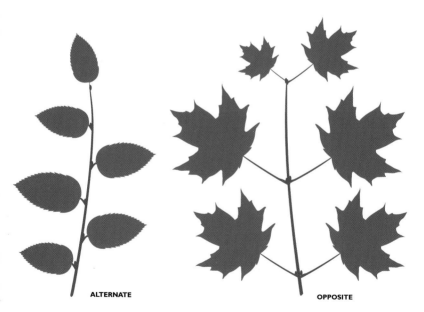

ALTERNATE   OPPOSITE

Alternate and Opposite Attachment
A key identifying feature for broad-leaved trees is whether the leaves are arranged alternately, like the hackberry (Celtis occidentalis) (left), or opposite, as with the sugar maple (Acer saccharum) (right).

LOOKING AT LEAVES

Leaf characteristics provide a number of clues to help identify a tree, including how the leaves are attached to the tree *(page opposite)*, leaf type (simple or compound), shape, and the details of their margins, or edges *(page 74)*.

Leaf arrangement may be alternate, growing one at a time from alternate sides of the twig, or opposite, growing in pairs, one on each side from the same place on the twig. A variation on opposite is whorled, in which more than two leaves grow from the same place. If you can't observe a twig with leaves attached, look at the way the twigs grow on the branches: The pattern of twig growth is the same as leaf growth.

With simple leaves, such as those of the elm (*Ulmus*) or the catalpa (*Catalpa*), the stalk of each leaf is attached directly to the twig. If a tree has compound leaves, such as the butternut (*Juglans cinerea*) or the buckeye (*Aesculus*), each leaf is made up of a number of leaflets attached to a single stem, which is attached to the twig.

Telling the two apart can be tricky, but a sure clue is the presence of buds. Both simple and compound leaves have a bud—called an axillary bud—just above where the leaf attaches to a twig. But there is no bud where the leaflet of a compound leaf attaches to the stem.

Compound leaves may be pinnately (feather) compound, with leaflets on each side of a central stem, or palmately compound, with the leaflets starting from the end of the stem, spreading out like a fan.

The shape of the leaf or leaflet provides a series of clues to tree identity. The form of the whole leaf may be described very specifically, with terms such as obovate (inverse egg-shaped), lanceolate (lance-shaped), or deltate (triangular). The shape of the leaf base, such as rounded or uneven, and the leaf tip, such as acute (like an acute angle) or truncate (appearing to be cut off abruptly), also help differentiate species.

Leaf margins—the edge of the leaf or leaflet—are also telltale clues. Margins can be smooth (called entire) or toothed. Among toothed leaves there are various types, including wavy, or crenate; finely toothed, or serrate; and deeply toothed, or dentate. And then there are leaves with teeth so pronounced that they form lobes. These lobes may be pointed or rounded and the sinus (indentation between the lobes) may also be pointed or rounded.

Grouping all of these characteristics together narrows down the options. For example, the butternut has compound leaves arranged oppositely. The leaflets are elliptical, with serrate margins. This description also applies to the black walnut (*Juglans nigra*), so to distinguish the two you must examine other features, such as the shape of the fruit: Butternuts are elliptical, while walnuts are rounder. Or, you can use the bark characteristics: Ridges in butternut bark are wider, smooth-topped, and shiny-dull, while those in walnut are dull.

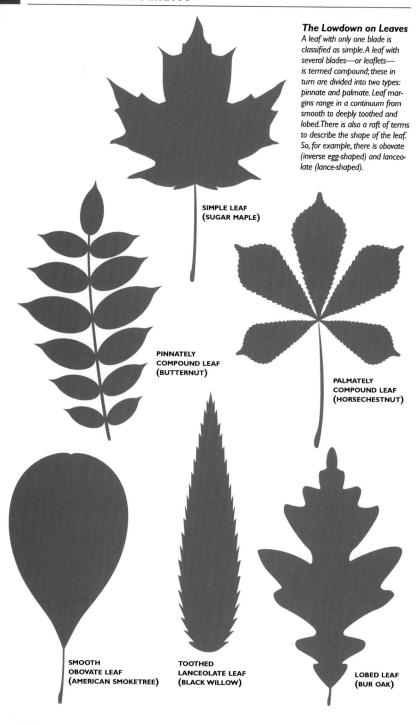

The Lowdown on Leaves
A leaf with only one blade is classified as simple. A leaf with several blades—or leaflets—is termed compound; these in turn are divided into two types: pinnate and palmate. Leaf margins range in a continuum from smooth to deeply toothed and lobed. There is also a raft of terms to describe the shape of the leaf. So, for example, there is obovate (inverse egg-shaped) and lanceolate (lance-shaped).

SIMPLE LEAF
(SUGAR MAPLE)

PINNATELY
COMPOUND LEAF
(BUTTERNUT)

PALMATELY
COMPOUND LEAF
(HORSECHESTNUT)

SMOOTH
OBOVATE LEAF
(AMERICAN SMOKETREE)

TOOTHED
LANCEOLATE LEAF
(BLACK WILLOW)

LOBED LEAF
(BUR OAK)

CLASSIFYING CONIFERS

Identifying conifers is easier than identifying broad-leaved trees, partly because there are fewer genera and species. Conifers are also distinguished by their leaf characteristics *(right)*. The first thing to look at is whether the leaves are scalelike (small and hugging the twig), as for junipers (*Juniperus*) and cedars (*Thuja*), or needlelike, as for other conifers. Needlelike leaves will either be clustered together on the twig, as for pines (*Pinus*) and tamaracks, or larches (*Larix*), or individual, as for firs (*Abies*), spruces (*Picea*), hemlocks (*Tsuga*), baldcypresses (*Taxodium*), and yews (*Taxus*).

The number of needles in the cluster is also important. Pines usually have bundles of two, three, or five, while tamaracks have many needles clustered together. Individual needles may be flat, four-sided, with or without a short stem, and may be arranged in flat sprays or around the twig.

SCALES
(ALASKA CEDAR)

SINGLE NEEDLES
(BALSAM FIR)

BUNDLED NEEDLES
(RED PINE)

CLUSTERED NEEDLES
(TAMARACK)

Needles and Scales
Conifers' "leaves" are either scalelike or needlelike. Some trees have single needles; other have needles arranged in bundles of two to five. The number in a bundle offers a clue to a species' identity. Red pine (Pinus resinosa), for example, has bundles of two, while the eastern white pine (Pinus strobus) has bundles of five. There are also needles arranged in a cluster.

THE WHOLE PICTURE

The list of clues useful in identifying trees is a long one, extending beyond the telltale leaves to include habit, bark texture and color, flowers and fruit or cones, presence or absence of spines, and so on.

Consider the shape of the tree. Can you follow the trunk by eye almost to the top of the crown or does it split into major branches fairly soon, making it hard to tell which branch is the main one in the crown? Is the crown roughly round or oval? Do the branches tend to curve up at the end or do they point more toward the ground? Species do have characteristic shapes, but there can be a great range of variation in individ-

ual trees. Whether the tree is growing in the open or in a forest, for example, can affect its habit. Forest-grown trees tend to have a longer length of straight trunk before the branches start and have a narrower or less-spreading crown. Recognizing characteristic tree shapes becomes easier with practice.

Look closely at the bark (below). What color is it: brown, gray, white, reddish? Is it smooth or rough, flaky, shaggy, or papery? For younger trees, which have not yet developed their mature bark, color is an important identifying feature and may be different from that of mature trees.

Finally, look at any other features you can. If the tree has cones, are they large or small? What shape

PAPER BIRCH

SHAGBARK HICKORY

BEECH

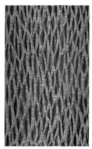

AMERICAN ASH

Bark Types

Examining bark type is a particularly helpful way to identify a particular species, especially when deciduous trees have lost their leaves. Some of the most common varieties are shown here: clockwise from top left, the papery texture of paper birch (Betula papyrifera), the shaggy look of shagbark hickory (Carya ovata), the leathery appearance of beech (Fagus grandifolia), the diamond pattern of American ash (Fraxinus americana), the stringy bark of white cedar (Thuja occidentalis), and the mottled texture of sycamore (Platanus occidentalis).

SYCAMORE

WHITE CEDAR

are they: roundish, elongated, curved? If you can see the flowers or fruit, take note of them, too. Like any detective work, the more clues you can amass about your quarry, the better your chance of making a positive ID.

KEYS TO TREE IDENTITY

One of the best tools for identifying an unknown tree is an identification key, which is a detailed list of the observable features a tree may or may not have, organized so the user is forced to select among alternatives. Most keys divide trees into broad groupings based on the leaves: their type, shape, arrangement on the twig, and margins, or edges. Specialized keys based on fruit or bark texture are sometimes used to differentiate between otherwise similar trees, while winter keys use characteristics such as details of twigs and buds that let you identify deciduous trees without their leaves.

To use a key, you compare the tree you're looking at with various descriptions in the book, answering a series of yes–no questions— usually in pairs of two—about the characteristics of the tree. Depending on the answer, you flip to another part of the book, respond to another pair of questions, and so on, until the choice is narrowed down.

Some guides make use of leaf characteristics alone to separate trees into fairly small groups since each tree has its own particular combination of the various options. You then flip through the descriptions, looking at other clues, such as bark texture, leaf texture, and fruit type, until you find the one that matches. Other guides continue the series of yes– no questions until a definitive identification is made.

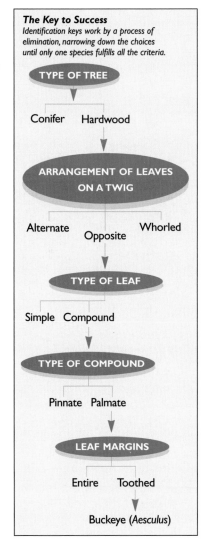

The Key to Success
Identification keys work by a process of elimination, narrowing down the choices until only one species fulfills all the criteria.

TYPE OF TREE

Conifer   Hardwood

ARRANGEMENT OF LEAVES ON A TWIG

Alternate   Whorled
        Opposite

TYPE OF LEAF

Simple   Compound

TYPE OF COMPOUND

Pinnate   Palmate

LEAF MARGINS

Entire   Toothed

Buckeye (*Aesculus*)

The Hands–on Naturalist

When they are out in the field, naturalists typically keep a record of their observations. You can, too. In addition to taking notes, the hands-on activities described here are creative ways to keep a permanent reminder of what you have seen. Even young children can enjoy bark rubbing and leaf pressing, while leaf printing and photography are good projects for older kids and adults.

a pile of books. Wait about a week for the leaves to dry completely before removing them. Instead of using books, you can buy a specially made leaf press, which is available at some craft stores. Not all leaves lend themselves to the procedure, however. For example, leathery leaves, such as those from magnolia trees (*Magnoliaceae*), tend not to dry well.

As you become handier with making leaf prints, try to get the impression of the entire leaf with a single pass of the roller. This will give you a more precise and delicate-looking print.

LEAF PRESSING

Instead of drying up and becoming discolored like leaves normally do, pressed leaves retain their shape and much of their color. Collect newly fallen leaves or cut fresh ones. Place the leaves between two pieces of paper towel or blotting paper, making sure they do not overlap, and lay them flat under

BARK RUBBING

To capture the patterns and textures of bark, rub a crayon or graphite art stick over a thick piece of paper pinned to a tree. The raised parts of the bark surface will leave corresponding marks on the paper. Record the name of the tree species on the sheet, as well as the date and other information, for future reference.

LEAF PRINTING

Leaf printing allows you to reproduce the beautiful symmetry of a leaf and its intricate network of veins in a style that resembles a wood cut. Green leaves with distinct veins, such as maple (*Acer*) and poplar (*Populus*), provide the best results. A more elaborate project than leaf pressing or bark rubbing, leaf printing requires two rubber hand rollers, printer's ink, and sheets of rice paper and plain paper. Your local craft store will probably carry these items.

Working on a sturdy surface, position a leaf—veined side up—on a sheet of plain paper, then place a few drops of ink on the leaf and spread it evenly on the surface with a roller. Transfer the leaf to a fresh sheet of plain paper, cover the inked side with a piece of rice paper, and carefully tape the two pieces together. Run the clean roller back and forth across the top sheet, pressing firmly. Peel the paper and the leaf apart and let the print dry.

Photographing Trees

In most cases, the best way to shoot a single tree is to turn your camera sideways for a vertical portrait shot that fills most of the frame. For a clear, uncluttered shot, look for trees that stand alone and are set off by a simple background, such as the sky, that contrasts with the tree in color or brightness. When possible, shoot from the same level as the tree; angling the camera up or down will make the top or bottom of the tree look unnaturally narrow. If you must tilt the camera to capture the top of a tall tree, avoid using a very wide-angle lens since this will exaggerate the distortion.

Lightly cloudy days are best for photographing trees. Always keep the sun behind you. If you shoot early or late in the day, the lower angle of the sun will light the full height of the tree, including the lower part of the trunk. Experiment with your camera's backlight feature, f-stop, light meter, and film types to get the best results. Film speeds of ASA 200 or lower yield pictures with more definition. And remember, higher shutter speeds or a tripod can compensate for an unsteady hand.

Bark rubbing is an easy way to reproduce the appearance of a tree's distinctive bark. Start with trees that have smoother bark before working up to the more difficult rougher, craggy surfaces.

Extreme Trees

The oldest life forms on the planet—more than four thousand years old—are gnarled, sun-bleached bristlecone pines (*Pinus longaeva*) in the southwestern United States. Not particularly tall—about sixty feet (18 m) at most—they have adapted to poor mountainside soil, a growing season only six weeks long, gale-force winds, and annual precipitation, mostly snow, of only twelve inches (30 cm). The wizened trees have needles that live for decades and dense, pest-resistant wood. It can take a whole century for a bristlecone to add just an inch (2.5 cm) of girth. Most remarkably, much of the tree dies back over time, leaving only a single branch and a strip of bark to maintain life.

Their longevity was discovered in 1957, when researcher Edmund Schulman dated a specimen, named Methuselah—still living today—at 4,723 years, a millennium older than giant sequoias (*Sequoiadendron giganteum*), formerly considered the world's longest-lived trees. In 1964 a graduate student cut down an even older specimen, Prometheus, thought to have been more than 4,950 years old, while trying to determine its age. This travesty led to tighter restrictions, although today the biggest threat to the bristlecones' survival comes not from scientists but from tourists and poachers who crave its dense, colorful wood.

The life span of trees such as the bristlecone pine (Pinus longaeva) (above) *and the giant sequoia (Sequoiadendron giganteum) are often limited by the soil they grow in. Many of these ancient trees topple because of erosion of the ground underneath them. The trees themselves often show no signs of disease or injury.*

THE BIGGEST AND THE TALLEST

The world's most massive trees are giant sequoias. Growing on the western slopes of California's Sierra Nevada, sequoias can live up to thirty-five hundred years. General Sherman, the largest sequoia by volume, measures 272 feet (83 m) tall, the trunk thirty-five feet (11 m) in diameter; it weighs nearly fourteen hundred tons—the equivalent of ten diesel-electric locomotives.

The extreme girth of the African baobab (Adansonia digitata) has long been noted. Nineteenth-century British explorer David Livingstone reported baobab trunks in which twenty to thirty men could easily lie down.

The world's tallest trees, coast redwoods (*Sequoia sempervirens*), are also found in California. In 1963 the National Geographical Society measured one tree—now known as the Society tree—at more than 364 feet (110 m). It weighs eight hundred tons. These skyscrapers belong to the same family as the giant sequoias.

GREAT GIRTH

The trunk of the world's largest Montezuma baldcypress, situated in a churchyard at Santa Maria de Tule near Oaxaca, Mexico, is 160 feet (49 m) in circumference. More than fifty people holding hands are needed to circle its girth. This two-thousand-year-old specimen has its own fan club called "My Friend the Tree," which has given the cypress a publicity lightning rod.

The trunk of the baobab (*Adansonia digitata*), which can measure up to thirty-three feet (10 m) in diameter, supports stunted, rootlike branches. Found on arid savannas, the baobab is part of African folklore. According to legend, it became disproportionately shaped because the gods tossed it into the air and it landed upside down. One large trunk can store twenty-five thousand gallons (110,000 l) of water, roughly equivalent to a backyard swimming pool. The soft wood is easily invaded by fungus and so large parts of the trunk become hollow. Sometimes human corpses were suspended in these hollows and became mummified. Remarkably, even when hollowed out, baobabs still flourish, sending out a root system three hundred feet (90 m) long.

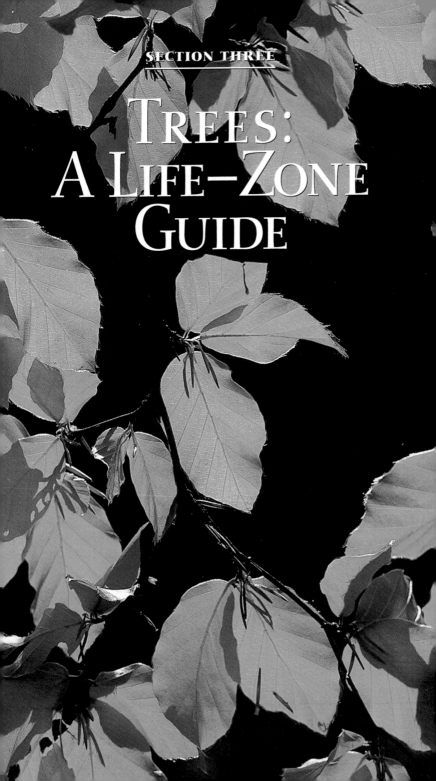

TREES:
A LIFE–ZONE
GUIDE

The Biomes & Their Trees

The following section offers illustrations and descriptions of 161 tree species from around the world. Some have been selected for inclusion because they are representative of their family or genus, others because they are unusual, rare, or economically important.

The trees are grouped according to biomes. A biome is generally defined as a major community of plants and animals that share similar environmental conditions. The seven biomes included here—temperate forest; tropical forest; northern boreal forest; rain forest; tidal zones, shores, and swamps; savanna and chaparral; and desert—encompass all the regions on the planet where trees grow. A description of each biome precedes the sampling of trees found in these areas.

While this is a useful way to set apart trees at a glance, some species in fact live in more than one biome.

- Temperate
- Tropical
- Northern Boreal
- Rain Forest
- Tidal Zones, Shores, & Swamps
- Savanna & Chaparral
- Desert

For example, a coniferous tree such as the eastern white pine (*Pinus strobus*), which is typically associated with boreal forests in Canada and the Appalachian Mountains of the United States, also can be found thousands of miles south in tropical forests at high elevations.

Species in this guide are assigned to the biome where they most often grow. The full extent of their range is noted, along with information about their traits, uses, and other points of interest.

Keep in mind that it is difficult to show on any one map precisely where a biome starts and ends. And sometimes biomes can exist within other biomes. In the case of the biome called tidal zones, shores, and swamps, no attempt has been made to chart the innumerable swamps that can be found around the world, from the Mekong Delta in Indochina to the Okefenokee Swamp in Georgia.

Temperate

The temperate biome has several distinct seasons over the course of the year, including a cold, dry winter during which tree growth stops. While conifers are not unusual in this life zone, deciduous broad-leaved angiosperms are much more common. Conifers remain green throughout the year because their needles are protected from desiccation by a wax coating and from freezing temperatures by certain chemicals. In contrast, broadleaf angiosperms shed their leaves to survive winter dormancy, a tactic that has allowed them to diversify and flourish. While fewer than five hundred conifer tree species exist in the entire world, more than a thousand angiosperm tree species are native to the temperate forests of North America alone.

THREE FOREST REGIONS

There are three primary temperate forest regions in the northern hemisphere. One occupies the eastern half of North America; another extends from western Europe through central Europe and eastward to the Caucasus; the third is found throughout most of eastern China. While these regions share many of the same families and genera of deciduous angiosperms, their native species differ, giving each region its own character.

Of the three regions, the two located farthest from each other—North America and China—share a higher number of families and genera than either does with Europe. For example, unlike North America and China, Europe has no native species of magnolia (*Magnoliaceae*), hickory (*Carya*), or sassafras (*Sassafras albidum*), despite growing conditions throughout much of Europe that would accommodate all three. This is a result of both geography and the effects of the Ice Age. The primary mountain ranges of Europe form an almost continuous barrier that extends east–west from Spain to the Caucasus. As a result, some of the families and genera of trees once found in Europe became extinct as the ice sheets advanced south. This did not occur in either China or North America because of the predominant north–south orientation of the major mountain ranges. The glaciation in the Orient was not as severe, but still the flora in these two regions were able to retreat from advancing glaciers and later retake their former territory when the ice receded.

OTHER FACTORS AT WORK

While geography and major geologic events like the Ice Age are powerful influences over a region's flora, plant diversity is also highly affected by more subtle and localized factors, such as soil type, elevation, and rainfall patterns. For example, the vast deciduous forest of eastern North America is actually a mosaic of many smaller environments distinguished by variations in the mix of species they contain. A river-plain forest in Ohio may be dominated by beech (*Fagus grandifolia*) and maple trees (*Acer*), while an upland forest in Tennessee may be characterized by yellow-poplar (*Lireodendron tulipifera*) and hickory (*Carya*) trees, but both are classified as temperate, North American deciduous forests.

DECIDUOUS VERSUS EVERGREEN

Towards its warmer extremes, the temperate zone is not purely deciduous. The moist, maritime climate of the Atlantic seaboard, from Maryland south to Georgia, accommodates live oak (*Quercus virginiana*), holly (*Ilex*), and a few other essentially evergreen angiosperms that are hardy enough to survive a cool winter season. On the other side of the continent, the more arid but equally moderate climate of Southern California supports forests on the coastal mountain ranges that vary according to elevation. Perhaps the most distinctive environment within a larger temperate forest is the coastal region of the Pacific Northwest. Although well north of the tropics and dominated by conifer species, the forest that grows here actually fulfills the environmental criteria of a rain forest *(page 150)*.

While temperate forests may not be as diverse as tropical rain forests, they still contain a broad range of species and a variety of distinct and productive forest types.

CRAB APPLE / *Malus coronaria*

This small, bushy fruit tree has a straight trunk and a spreading, rounded crown. It favors moist soil and in the wild several trees often grow together in thickets. In May or June, the tree produces delicate, five-petaled blossoms that contrast with the sharp spines that distinguish the branchlets. In the late autumn, it produces small, yellow-green apples. The lovely rose-colored blossoms and their spicy fragrance make this small fruit tree a popular ornamental. The tart fruit is used for cider and jellies.

Size: Grows as high as 30 feet (9 m), with diameter of about 14 inches (35 cm)

Range: Concentrated in Pennsylvania, Ohio, and Indiana, but also scattered farther south and west in U.S.

Other common names: Sweet crabapple

AMERICAN ASH / *Fraxinus americana*

Size: Typically grows to 80 feet (24 m) and occasionally higher, with diameter of up to 5 feet (1.5 m) or more

Range: Eastern U.S. and Canada

Other common names: White ash

This species is the tallest of the North American ashes and the most important one in the timber industry. It is used for veneer and paneling, and its strong, tough, relatively light wood is a favorite for tool handles and baseball bats. The ash tree grows to medium height and has a straight trunk and sturdy branches. The leaves grow in featherlike groups of leaflets and turn purple in the fall. The trees are either male or female. On male trees the flowers grow in dense clusters, while on the female tree they appear in looser sprays. The tree's winged seeds can be carried long distances by the wind.

AMERICAN BASSWOOD / *Tilia americana*

Basswood is a fast-growing deciduous tree with large, heart-shaped leaves. In midsummer it bears clusters of tiny, white, extremely fragrant flowers that develop into nutlike fruits. Bees are fond of the flowers, which produce an abundance of nectar from which a choice honey is made. Basswood is a longtime favorite as a shade tree in urban areas and is also an important timber tree. It has a relatively soft wood that is valued for hand carving and the inner bark, or bast, can be used as a source of fiber for making rope or for weaving such items as baskets and mats.

Size: Reaches height of 75 to 130 feet (23 to 40 m), with diameter of 36 to 50 inches (90 to 125 cm)

Range: Northeastern U.S. and southeastern Canada

Other common names: Linden

BEECH / *Fagus grandifolia*

Size: Height generally 60 to 80 feet (16 to 24 m), with some growing as tall as 120 feet (37 m)

Range: Lower elevations throughout most of eastern North America

Other common names: American beech

A forest grove of beech trees is a dark and eerie place. The thick foliage of these massive deciduous trees lets almost no light reach the forest floor. In the deep shade, practically nothing will grow. The leaves have the unusual characteristic of often clinging to the branches until they are replaced by new ones in the spring. Beech trees are slow-growing, but can spread themselves with sucker roots, resulting in groves of trees clustered together.

BOXELDER / *Acer negundo*

The compound leaves of this member of the maple family look so much like those of the ash that the tree is sometimes referred to as the ash-leaved maple. On closer inspection, the flowers and the double-winged seeds are typically maple. A remarkably hardy tree, the boxelder grows almost everywhere in North America and is so common that in some places it is considered no more valuable than a weed. It has fallen out of favor as a city tree because it drops a huge quantity of seeds and harbors many insects. Unlike some members of the maple family, the soft, weak wood of the boxelder is rarely used by woodworkers.

Size: Grows 50 to 75 feet (15 to 23 m) high, with diameter of roughly 3 feet (1 m)

Range: Southern Canada and much of continental U.S., except most of Florida and far western states

Other common names: Ash-leaved maple

BUTTERNUT / *Juglans cinerea*

Size: Generally grows 40 to 60 feet (12 to 18 m) tall, but sometimes reaches height of 100 feet (30 m)

Range: From western Canada south to North Carolina and west to Minnesota

Other common names: White walnut, oilnut

A close cousin of the black walnut, the butternut is somewhat shorter, with bark that is gray rather than dark brown. Like the walnut, the butternut yields sweet-tasting nuts that are popular with both people and wildlife. The nut husks were used by the pioneers to dye overalls a golden brown; this article of clothing became known as "butternut jeans." The inner bark of the butternut was once used by doctors as a cathartic. Unfortunately, this handsome species has recently become threatened by a fungal disease that has killed up to 80 percent of the trees in some parts of its range.

CALIFORNIA-LAUREL / *Umbellularia californica*

Size: Usually a shrub or small tree, 40 to 80 feet (12 to 24 m) tall

Range: Western U.S.

Other common names: Myrtlewood, bay, Oregon myrtle, spice tree

A small, broad-leaved evergreen, the California-laurel has long, thick, leathery leaves that are very aromatic when crushed. Loose clusters of small yellowish green flowers appear in winter or early spring. The round fruits are greenish to purple. The wood, usually marketed as myrtlewood, is hard, beautifully grained, and takes a high polish, making it suitable for decorative items, such as furniture and gun stocks, while burls with unusual grains are especially prized for inlays. The leaves, seeds, and wood have strong chemical properties and have traditionally been used by Native Americans to treat a variety of complaints. The California-laurel is grown both indoors and outdoors as an ornamental.

NORTHERN CATALPA / *Catalpa speciosa*

This tall deciduous tree is easy to identify by its distinctive leaves, flowers, and seeds. The large, heart-shaped leaves can be as long as ten inches (25 cm). New leaves are a soft purple color. The flowers resemble snowy white bells; they are flecked at the center with purple and yellow and hang in clusters. After the flowers die, long seed pods grow. These have earned the tree the common name Indian bean tree. The northern catalpa is often planted as an ornamental, but its wood is weak, making the tree particularly vulnerable in storms. Still, the wood is sometimes used for fence posts and in cabinetry.

Size: Up to 100 feet (30 m) in height

Range: Restricted native region of southern Illinois south to Tennessee and Arkansas; now widely planted outside original range

Other common names: Indian bean tree

CEDAR OF LEBANON / *Cedrus libani*

The cedar of Lebanon is highly regarded as an ornamental in many temperate regions of the world. It is a very large tree with both horizontal and uplifted branches and foliage that resembles that of the larch. Needles are on short shoots, with thirty to forty needles to a tuft. The cones are oblong and resinous, and sit upright on the branches. The wood has been prized since antiquity and is mentioned in the Old Testament. Because of its durability, sweet scent, and color, it was used in ancient Egyptian temples and was also a favorite material of shipbuilders. The tree is slow-growing and may live a thousand years.

Size: Up to 165 feet (50 m) tall, with diameter of 10 feet (3 m); wide umbrella shape at maturity

Range: Native to Turkey and Lebanon, but widely cultivated

BLACK CHERRY / *Prunus serotina*

Size: Grows to height of 100 feet (30 m) and diameter of up to 5 feet (1.5 m)

Range: Widespread through eastern North America and south to Guatemala

The black cherry is the largest of the wild cherries of North America and the most widespread. Less ornamental than many of the imported Asian cherries, it produces unremarkable spikes of white flowers. The fruit is small and somewhat bitter, enjoyed more often by birds and small animals than by humans. The true value of the tree to people lies in the gorgeous luster of its red-brown wood, making it one of the most prestigious hardwoods of North America. In addition to its use in fine furniture and interior trim, the exceptionally stable wood was once used for type blocks in printing.

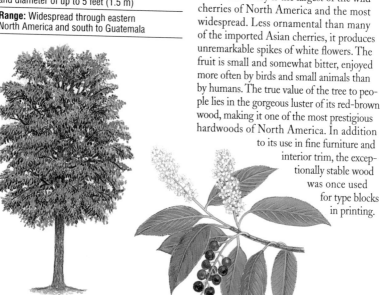

AMERICAN CHESTNUT / *Castanea dentata*

Size: Average height used to be about 105 feet (32 m), but today rarely exceeds 30 feet (9 m)

Range: Northeastern U.S. and southeastern Ontario

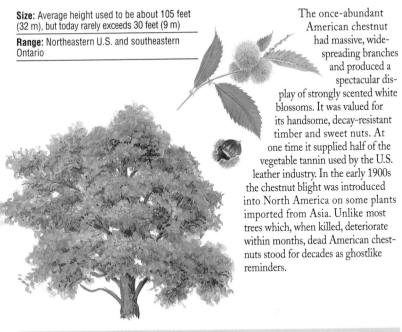

The once-abundant American chestnut had massive, wide-spreading branches and produced a spectacular display of strongly scented white blossoms. It was valued for its handsome, decay-resistant timber and sweet nuts. At one time it supplied half of the vegetable tannin used by the U.S. leather industry. In the early 1900s the chestnut blight was introduced into North America on some plants imported from Asia. Unlike most trees which, when killed, deteriorate within months, dead American chestnuts stood for decades as ghostlike reminders.

EASTERN COTTONWOOD / *Populus deltoides*

The eastern cottonwood is one of the largest and fastest-growing hardwoods of the eastern United States. The leaves are shiny green and triangular with rounded teeth. Early in the spring, small, greenish flowers droop in long clusters, called catkins, and form masses of seeds. Each seed is attached to a tuft of cottony hairs and although some are blown away by the wind, most fall down and accumulate in a thick, fluffy layer under the tree. The rapid growth of the eastern cottonwood and its light, soft wood make it valuable commercially. The tree thrives in moist soils and it is frequently planted to provide quick shade near buildings.

Size: Trees average 100 feet (30 m) in height and 3 feet (1 m) in diameter

Range: Eastern U.S. and southern Canada

Other common names: Eastern poplar, southern cottonwood, Carolina poplar

MONTEREY CYPRESS / *Cupressus macrocarpa*

This small conifer is restricted in the wild to two points along the coast of Monterey County in California. Clinging to cliffs and bluffs, it grows in a stunted and contorted shape, its branches resembling antlers. The needles are scalelike and the cones are neat little globes. The sight of the eccentric trees against an ocean backdrop has made them a favorite with artists and photographers. The Monterey cypress is a very popular garden tree. Away from the ocean winds, it is less contorted, but can still grow in a variety of forms, including a full-spreading dome that resembles a cedar of Lebanon.

Size: 15 to 80 feet (4 to 24 m) tall, with diameter of up to 4 feet (1.3 m)

Range: Restricted to coast of Monterey County in California

FLOWERING DOGWOOD / *Cornus florida*

Size: Low branching, 20 to 25 feet (6 to 7.5 m) tall

Range: Eastern U.S., southern Canada, northern Mexico

Other common names: Boxwood, cornel

The blossoms of the flowering dogwood provide a spectacular display in the spring and are so hardy that they often stay colorful for three to four weeks—twice as long as blossoms on other trees. The species name is Latin for flowering, but the showy, petal-like blossoms are not in fact flowers, but bracts—a specialized type of leaves. The bracts are usually white, although pink and red varieties exist, and each has a distinctive notch at its tip. Small clusters of bright red berries, borne on the end of the twigs, are poisonous to humans, but provide a great variety of wildlife with food. The bark is nearly black and on old trunks is deeply furrowed in a checkerboard pattern.

AMERICAN ELM / *Ulmus americana*

This beloved and stately tree was once a familiar sight in virtually every town in the northeastern United States. Its tall, vaselike shape made it ideal for shading busy streets. Tragically, the American elm has been all but wiped out by Dutch elm disease, a fungal disease spread by beetles. The disease was first introduced into North America in 1930 via shipments of imported lumber and gradually spread across the country. The fungus grows within the living tissues of the tree and cuts off the flow of sap. Only a costly program of spraying and injecting individual trees can save them. Once infected, a two-hundred-year-old tree can be killed in a single season. Fortunately, the American elm still survives in some woodlands and along stream banks.

Size: Generally 65 to 100 feet (20 to 30 m) tall, but can reach height of up to 130 feet (40 m); diameter ranges from 3 to 10 feet (1 to 3 m)

Range: Throughout eastern North America

GINKGO / *Ginkgo biloba*

Size: Can grow as tall as 120 feet (35 m), but generally reaches height of 50 to 80 feet (15 to 25 m)

Range: Cultivated in Europe, Asia, the U.S., and southern Canada; grows naturally in only two small mountainous areas of China, possibly offspring of ginkgoes grown in temple gardens

The ginkgo is a deciduous gymnosperm tree with gray bark and tough, fan-shaped leaves. The fruit is mildly toxic and has an obnoxious odor when it falls off the tree and starts to decompose. Ginkgo trees evolved more than 200 million years ago. Fossils of leaves found in the United States show that ginkgoes disappeared from North America about seven million years ago, but they have recently been reintroduced. Ginkgoes are popular in urban areas due to their resistance to air pollution and disease. The seeds and leaves are thought to have medicinal value. In China and Japan, the tree is considered sacred and is grown in temple gardens.

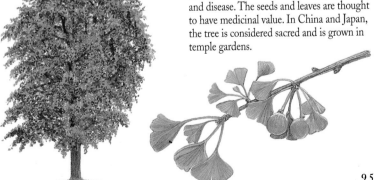

HACKBERRY / *Celtis occidentalis*

Opinions are mixed over whether this small deciduous tree of the elm family is an appropriate city tree. While its ability to stand up to droughts makes the hackberry tree a common choice in midwestern towns, some find the tree messy and unattractive and would like to see other trees take its place. To begin with, the tree's gray-brown corky bark is covered with irregular, wartlike protrusions. In addition, a common tree disease causes clusters of twigs, called witches brooms, to grow from the trunk and eventually litter the ground. The hackberry is named for the abundant small, round fruits it produces, which resemble dark-purple cherries.

Size: Grows to height of 30 to 50 feet (9 to 15 m)

Range: Eastern Canada and U.S. as far south as Oklahoma

ENGLISH HAWTHORN / *Crataegus laevigata*

Size: May attain height of 30 feet (9 m)

Range: Native to Europe and northern Africa, but naturalized to North America

A remarkably tough tree that can endure seasons of drought and cold, the English hawthorn is also noted for its beauty in the spring. The white, pink, or red flowers are borne in showy clusters much like those of the apple tree. The leaves are lobed and conspicuously toothed and change to scarlet or yellow in the autumn. Hawthorn trees have many spines and are ideally suited as hedges. They not only withstand heavy pruning, but form a dense interlacing network of twigs that is almost impenetrable. The attractive red fruit, called a haw, has a dry, mealy pulp, and hawthorn berry extracts have been used historically as a cardiac tonic.

ENGLISH HOLLY / *Ilex aquifolium*

A familiar symbol of Christmas, English holly has dark, glossy leaves that contrast dramatically with its bright-red berries. Because the holly's female and male flowers are produced by different trees, male and female trees must grow within about a hundred feet (30 m) of each other to consistently produce berries. The English holly has long been revered in the British Isles, where the tree was once believed to have the power to ward off evil; it was considered unlucky to cut one down. The Irish referred to the holly as "the gentle tree" and believed it was the favorite of fairies.

Size: Up to 80 feet (24 m) high

Range: Britain and Ireland

HONEYLOCUST / *Gleditsia triacanthos*

Size: In natural stands, generally 65 to 80 feet (20 to 24 m) high and 24 to 36 inches (60 to 90 cm) in diameter

Range: Scattered in east-central U.S.; cultivated as ornamental in all countries having temperate climate

Other common names: Sweet locust, thorny locust

A fast-growing deciduous tree, the honey-locust is hardy and tolerant of drought and salinity. The branches and often the trunk are armed with branched spines, although a thornless variety is often planted to replace the elm in many urban areas. The trees are also widely grown for windbreaks and erosion control. The compound leaves are composed of many leaflets and turn pale yellow in the autumn. Since the leaves tend to disintegrate as they drop, making raking unnecessary, honeylocusts are considered good yard trees. The seed pods are reddish brown with oval seeds in a succulent pulp, which is often consumed by live-stock and wildlife.

EASTERN HOPHORNBEAM / *Ostrya virginiana*

A small deciduous tree with elmlike leaves, the eastern hophornbeam belongs to a different genus than its cousin, the American hornbeam. It owes its name to its seeds, which hang in clusters and resemble hops. The seeds are preceded by male and female flowers that grow as catkins; female catkins stand up and male ones hang. The wood of the hophornbeam is so hard that the tree, along with the American hornbeam, is often referred to as ironwood. Although the hophornbeam is too small for its wood to be used commercially, Native Americans had a number of uses for the wood, including for framing dwellings.

Size: Generally grows to about 40 feet (12 m) in height, taller in certain regions

Range: Throughout eastern North America as far south as Florida

Other common names: Ironwood

HORSECHESTNUT / *Aesculus hippocastanum*

Size: Typically 80 to 100 feet (25 to 30 m) tall, with diameter of 5 feet (1.5 m)

Range: Native to Asia and southeastern Europe, but used as ornamental throughout central North America

The formal pyramidal top of the horsechestnut is a familiar sight in the parks and along the roadsides of many urban areas throughout the world. For two weeks in late spring, showy spikes of white flowers mottled with red sit erect at the end of the branches. The polished dark chestnut-brown nuts—often called conkers—have a prickly, green husk. Both the leaves and the nuts are poisonous to humans, but the nuts are much sought after by squirrels, cattle, and deer. A compound called esculin is obtained from the bark and leaves for use in cosmetics to prevent sunburn. The horsechestnut is in a family of its own and is not closely related to the American chestnut.

JARRAH / *Eucalyptus marginata*

The jarrah is a tall tree unique to western Australia with an international reputation as one of the finest general-purpose hardwoods in the world. The color of the wood ranges from salmon-pink to rich, reddish brown. Because the wood is hard and resistant to termites, marine borers, rot, and fire, it is used for railway sleepers, bridge and dock piles, and heavy construction, as well as for cabinetmaking. At one time it even served as paving blocks in the streets of London. The fibrous bark changes from red-brown to gray as the tree ages. The jarrah grows well in almost any well-drained soil in Australia, although attempts made to grow it in other parts of the world have been unsuccessful.

Size: Up to 130 feet (40 m) in height, with diameter of 7 feet (2 m); in poor conditions, such as stony slopes, may grow only 7 feet (2 m) tall

Range: Coastal belt of southwest Australia

BLACK LOCUST / *Robinia pseudoacacia*

Size: Grows 50 to 65 feet (15 to 20 m) tall, with diameter of 12 to 30 inches (30 to 75 cm)

Range: Originally localized in part of eastern U.S.; has been planted widely, becoming naturalized throughout U.S., southern Canada, and parts of Europe and Asia

Other common names: Yellow locust, false acacia

This fast-growing, spindly tree can thrive in poor, dry soil. It has thorns at the base of its fernlike leaves and produces clusters of fragrant, pealike flowers that are generally white, although pink ornamental varieties exist. Black locust is used as fuel and pulp; its hardwood, which swells very little in water, is also valued for making insulator pins and tree nails for wooden ship construction. Because the tree grows rapidly and the roots transform nitrogen from the air into nitrogen-containing minerals in the ground, black locust is widely planted as an ornamental, for erosion control, and the reclamation of drastically disturbed sites. Forest managers consider it a weed species because it competes strongly against more desirable species.

PACIFIC MADRONE / *Arbutus menziesii*

Common along the length of the western coast of North America, the Pacific madrone is the largest member of the heath family. It is a small- to medium-sized broadleaf evergreen with a twisted and scraggly trunk and peeling, reddish bark. In the spring, it produces abundant tiny, jug-shaped flowers that attract honeybees. The red, berrylike fruit that follows contrasts strikingly with the dark leaves and is a favorite food of birds and small animals. The Pacific madrone has an interesting adaptive peculiarity. Before the leaf buds burst open, they exude a drop of sugary liquid, which attracts insects, deterring deer from devouring the new leaves.

Size: Generally grows 30 to 40 feet (9 to 12 m) tall, but can reach 130 feet (40 m) in redwood forests; diameter of 20 to 45 inches (50 to 110 cm)

Range: Pacific coast of North America, from southern British Columbia into southern California

SOUTHERN MAGNOLIA / *Magnolia grandiflora*

Size: Grows 60 to 80 feet (18 to 24 m) tall, with diameter of 2 to 3 feet (0.6 to 1 m)

Range: Southeast U.S. as far north as Alabama

Other common names: Bull-bay

Originally a native of the lowlands of the southeastern United States, the southern magnolia boasts large, fragrant white flowers that have made it a popular ornamental tree around the world. It is a tall evergreen with broad, thick, leathery leaves. The bottom of the leaves, as well as the young branches and the buds, are covered with distinctive rust-colored hairs. The showy flowers have nine to fourteen thick, creamy white petals, up to five inches (12 cm) long. The conelike fruit is also unique: Each bright red seed is suspended from the fruit on a hairlike strand, looking like a dangling earring.

NORWAY MAPLE / Acer platanoides

Highly sought-after as an ornamental species, the Norway maple grows rapidly into a handsome tree that casts a welcome shade on hot summer days. The five-lobed leaves are very similar to those of the sugar maple, but are distinguished by the drops of milky substance produced at the base of the leaf stems when they are plucked. Norway maples grow easily under a variety of conditions and can tolerate the polluted air of cities and the wind and salt spray of the seashore. A number of ornamental varieties of Norway maple differ widely from the ordinary species. For example, the crimson king maple has leaves of rich maroon color during the entire growing season.

Size: Generally grows 80 to 100 feet (24 to 30 m) in height, with rounded dome shape

Range: Native to Europe from Norway south and east as far as Russia; frequently planted as ornamental in North America

SILVER MAPLE / Acer saccharinum

Size: Grows to maximum height of about 100 feet (30 m), with diameter of 5 feet (1.5 m)

Range: Eastern North America as far south as Alabama

The silver maple is native to the lowlands of much of the eastern United States, thriving in the moist soil of riverbeds and along lakes. Its winged seeds are the largest of any of the North American maples and are a popular food for rodents, foxes, and birds. Heart rot often hollows out the branches and trunk, providing homes for squirrels and raccoons. The silver maple was once popular as a street tree, but has fallen out of favor because of its tendency to split. Its wood is sold as "soft maple" and is less valuable than that of the red or sugar maple.

SUGAR MAPLE / *Acer saccharum*

This tall, handsome maple is one of the most common trees of the deciduous forests of eastern North America and one of the most useful to people. Its wood is sold as "hard maple"—much more valuable than the softer wood of its cousin, the silver maple—and is used for everything from furniture and cabinetry to musical instruments. This species is also the primary source of maple syrup. The trees are tapped in the spring and the clear, watery sap is then boiled to reduce it to syrup. As much as thirty gallons (115 l) of sap is required to make a single gallon (4 l) of syrup.

Size: Grows 90 to 100 feet (27 to 30 m) tall, with diameter of up to about 3 feet (1 m)

Range: Eastern U.S. and Canada south to Tennessee

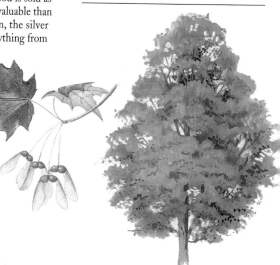

MONKEY-PUZZLE /*Araucaria araucana*

Size: Up to 100 feet (30 m) high

Range: Native to Andes of Chile and southwest Argentina; planted as ornamental in parts of North America

Other common names: Chile pine

The monkey-puzzle tree is covered in stiff, triangular, dark-green leaflike scales that clothe the branches so closely that they look like massive green ropes dipping down from the trunk and then up at the tips. The leathery leaves have a very sharp tip that points up; it is said that a monkey can climb up this tree but not down, hence its common name. Pollen and seed cones are on separate trees. The monkey-puzzle tree is a valuable timber tree in Argentina and Chile. Its trunk is straight and free from knots, yielding a beautifully grained, yellowish white wood and abundant resin.

RED MULBERRY / *Morus rubra*

The red mulberry is a rapid-growing deciduous tree. During summer it bears large, sweet fruits that resemble elongated blackberries. The berries, which turn from red to purple when ripe, are used in jellies, jams, pies, and drinks. They are also a favorite of birds and small mammals and at one time were used for fattening hogs and as poultry food. Birds are so fond of the fruit that mulberry trees are sometimes planted near more valuable trees, such as cherries, to lure the birds away. Fruitless male trees are often grown or planted near paved areas to avoid the staining caused by fallen fruit. The oval leaves often have two or three lobes and their underside is covered in a soft fuzz.

Size: Ranges in height from 15 to 70 feet (5 to 20 m) depending on habitat conditions

Range: Eastern U.S

Other common names: Moral

COAST LIVE OAK / *Quercus agrifolia*

Size: From 30 to 80 feet (9 to 24 m) in height

Range: Along Pacific coast from San Francisco to Baja in California

Other common names: California live oak

The live oak of the U.S. west coast earned its name because, unlike the oaks of the east, it is an evergreen tree. Its leaves are dark and glossy with spiny edges and resemble the leaves of the holly tree. Although they stay on the tree for only a year or two, the leaves fall a few at a time, keeping the tree green year-round. The live oak often spreads much wider than its height, making it a popular shade tree in gardens, in parks, and along streets. In the wild, the coast live oak grows in pure stands on lower mountain slopes, in valleys, and on coastal islands.

CORK OAK / *Quercus suber*

This evergreen oak is native to the western Mediterranean basin and has evolved a unique way to survive the region's frequent droughts, forest fires, and swings in temperature. As the bark grows, it forms protective cork—a tough, flexible layer that is both waterproof and airtight. The light, spongy material is used for a range of products, from wine-bottle stoppers to flooring. The trees must be about fifty years old before the cork can be harvested, and it is then stripped only every ten years or so. Special hatchets are used to carefully pry off the bark, leaving the living inner layer unharmed. Portugal is the world's primary producer of cork.

Size: From 60 to 100 feet (18 to 30 m) tall, with diameter of up to 5 feet (1.5 m)

Range: Western Mediterranean basin

ENGLISH OAK / *Quercus robur*

Size: Up to 150 feet (45 m) tall, with diameter of up to 10 feet (3 m)

Range: From northern Europe to North Africa and into western Asia

This majestic tree is the most widely distributed oak in Europe. In colonial times it was brought to North America, where it was widely cultivated. The English oak has a short trunk and a broadly spreading crown. It can take on a contorted shape when growing alone. A symbol of wisdom and age throughout northern Europe, the English oak can live for many centuries. In times gone by, the tough, durable wood was particularly prized for shipbuilding and for the interiors of castles and churches.

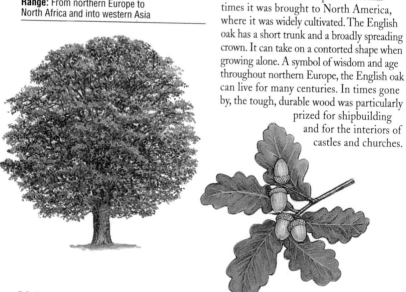

RED OAK / *Quercus rubra*

The red oak is an attractive, medium-sized deciduous tree with stout branches and dense foliage. Like other oaks, the female and male flowers look completely different from each other:
The female flowers grow in inconspic-uous clusters at the leaf junctions, while the male ones hang down as long catkins. The tree gets its descriptive name from the color of its wood. A pop-ular shade tree, the red oak is resis-tant to urban pollution and has been widely planted in Europe.

Size: Grows 65 to 100 feet (20 to 30 m) tall, with diameter of 2 to 3 feet (0.6 to 1 m)

Range: Eastern U.S. from New England south to Alabama; cultivated throughout Europe

OLIVE / *Olea europaea*

Size: Reaches height of 30 feet (9 m), with diameter of up to 2 feet (0.6 m)

Range: Common to entire Mediterranean region

Along with the yew, the olive is Europe's longest-lived tree, sometimes surviving fifteen hundred years. Olive trees even look ancient, with their gnarled trunk and silvery green leaves. The fruit starts out firm and green, wrinkling and turning purple as it ripens; it is inedible fresh. The oil pressed from the ripe fruit has made these trees a mainstay of the economy of the Mediterranean world since ancient times—and, indeed, the borders of the region could even be said to be defined by the range of the olive tree. Today the graceful olive branch, such as the one that the dove brought back to Noah on the ark, is a universal symbol of peace.

OSAGE ORANGE / *Maclura pomifera*

The Osage orange is a medium-sized thorny tree commonly used for hedges. The short, thick trunk divides into a few large limbs that send out curved branches. The lower branches and twigs have straight, sharp thorns. The bark is deeply furrowed and orange-brown in color, and the wood inside is hard and bright orange. Male and female flowers are on separate trees. If both trees are present, the female trees bear fruits, which have a bumpy, green and golden-yellow surface and resemble oranges. However, the fruit of the Osage orange is inedible and filled with a milky juice. The flexible wood was used by the Osage people of the Arkansas River region to make bows.

Size: From 30 to 50 feet (9 to 15 m) high, with diameter of up to 3 feet (1 m)

Range: Originally native to small area in southwestern U.S., but hedge plantings have extended range

ROYAL PAULOWNIA / *Paulownia tomentosa*

Size: Height at maturity ranges from 30 to 65 feet (9 to 20 m)

Range: Native to China, but introduced worldwide; limited to areas where temperature does not drop below -5° Fahrenheit (-20°C)

Other common names: Princess tree, empress tree

A fast-growing deciduous tree, the royal paulownia is strikingly beautiful in blossom. The vanilla-scented flowers, in violet or blue clusters, appear in April or May. The leaves of a mature tree are normally large—five to twelve inches (12 to 30 cm) long—and on young plants or fast-growing stems, they may measure almost three feet (1 m) in length and be nearly as wide. In North America, royal paulownia is grown as an ornamental, but its ability to establish on disturbed, exposed sites has made it a favorite for surface-mine reclamation. The wood of *Paulownia tomentosa* figures prominently in Oriental cultures, where it is used for making ceremonial boxes.

PAWPAW / *Asimina triloba*

Unrelated to the pawpaws of the tropics, the American pawpaw is actually a member of the custard apple family. It is a small, deciduous tree with large, drooping leaves that give it a tropical appearance. The flowers are an unusual maroon color with two whorls each of three petals. The thick, greenish-brown fruit grows up to six inches (15 cm) long and is, in fact, the largest native fruit of North America. Although appreciated by possums, raccoons, and other small animals, this fruit gets mixed reviews from human consumers. Some find it nauseating, while others describe its flavor as a pleasant mix of custard and banana.

Size: Grows 15 to 30 feet (5 to 9 m) high, with diameter of 4 to 12 inches (10 to 30 cm)

Range: Southeastern U.S. as far north as Pennsylvania

PEACH / *Prunus persica*

Size: Grows about 16 feet (5 m) tall; spread of 16 feet (5 m) gives rounded form

Range: Originally from China, but cultivated worldwide in temperate regions

The many varieties of peach trees are widely cultivated for their delicious fruits and beautiful blossoms in spring. The color of the fruit ranges from yellow to maroon, and the pulp is sweet, juicy, and golden and can be eaten raw or cooked. A popular variety of *Prunus persica* with no fuzz on the fruit is called the nectarine. Trees that are bred for their blossoms often have double flowers with numerous overlapping petals. Flowers are borne in great white, pink, or red clusters that mass along the stems or drop beneath them. A delightful variety called peppermint stick has white petals marked with pink and red stripes.

The leaves, twigs, and seeds of peach trees contain varying concentrations of a cyanide compound that is toxic to humans.

PECAN / *Carya illinoinensis*

Famous for the delicious nuts that they produce, pecan trees grow in areas with long, hot summers. The oval nuts turn from green to black as they ripen in the autumn. Pecan orchard trees are usually grown by grafting branch buds from trees that bear fine-quality nuts onto seedling stock. Trees grow slowly. It takes twenty years before they reach maturity, producing up to five hundred pounds (230 kg) of nuts each year.

Size: Can reach 180 feet (55 m) in height and up to 70 inches (180 cm) in diameter

Range: Southeastern U.S., Texas, and Mexico; cultivars grown in other countries where climate suitable

COMMON PERSIMMON / *Diospyros virginiana*

Size: Grows 30 to 60 feet (9 to 18 m), occasionally as tall as 80 feet (24 m); diameter up to 24 inches (60 cm)

Range: Southeastern U.S. as far north as southern New York

Growing by the road or alongside fences and the edges of fields, the common persimmon is a familiar sight throughout the southeastern United States. Its bark is its most distinctive feature. Regular fissures running vertically and horizontally divide the smoky gray trunk into a regular grid of rectangular blocks. The flowers are greenish yellow or white bells and the small, globular fruits range from orange to purple. Unlike the fruit of its Chinese cousin, the fruit of the American persimmon is so bitter it makes the lips pucker. It can only be eaten after the first frost when it is wrinkled and somewhat sweeter.

LOBLOLLY PINE / *Pinus taeda*

The loblolly is the tallest and fastest-growing of the pines of the southeastern United States. It tolerates a variety of soil conditions and springs up quickly in abandoned fields. In the forest, it is found both in pure stands and mixed in with other trees. The slender, pale green needles grow in groups of three. Both the needles and cones can be up to nine inches (23 cm) long. The abundant seeds are an important food source for birds and rodents. The tree's wood is coarse-grained and not as strong or durable as some southern pines; its uses are restricted to general construction and pulp.

Size: From 80 to 140 feet (24 to 42 m) tall, with diameter of 18 to 36 inches (45 to 90 cm)

Range: Southeastern U.S. and as far north as New Jersey along coast

LONGLEAF PINE / *Pinus palustris*

Size: Grows 100 to 130 feet (30 to 37 m) high, with diameter of 2 to 3 feet (0.6 to 1 m)

Range: Coastal plains of southeastern U.S.

Longleaf pines grow on sand hills and scrublands of the American southeast. The needles, clustered in tufts at the ends of the branchlets, can grow to eighteen inches (45 cm) long, giving the species its name. The longleaf pine has a unique growth pattern: It spends its first three to four years huddled as a low mound, referred to as the "grass stage." Only after it has put down a vigorous root system does it begin to grow upward to become a stately conifer. The tree's wood belongs to the species group termed "southern yellow pine," used in general construction and, as treated wood, for outdoor use.

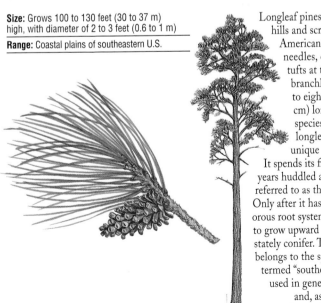

PONDEROSA PINE / *Pinus ponderosa*

The ponderosa pine dominates the forests of much of western North America. It owes its abundance and broad range to its toleration of a variety of elevations and soil types. A tall, straight conifer with few lower branches, its bark is a distinctive pinkish or orange color with clear fissures. The needles grow in tight, round bundles at the edge of the branchlets and the number of needles in a bundle helps define the variety. The seeds in the woody cones are an important food for birds and animals. The ponderosa pine is one of the most important timber trees of the west and its wood is used for everything from toys and furniture to general construction.

Size: Generally reaches 90 to 130 feet (27 to 40 m), but heights of 230 feet (70 m) recorded; diameter of 30 to 50 inches (75 to 125 cm)

Range: Scattered throughout much of western U.S. and north into southern British Columbia

SUGAR PINE / *Pinus lambertiana*

Size: Typically 165 to 195 feet (50 to 60 m) tall, sometimes reaching height of 245 feet (75 m)

Range: Western U.S. from sea level to elevation of 10,000 feet (3,000 m)

The tallest of the American pines, the magnificent sugar pine is named for the sugary sap that seeps from the tree through cuts in the bark. The cones of the sugar pine are the largest of any American conifer, measuring from twelve to twenty-two inches (30 to 56 cm) in length. The tree's blue-green needles are long and flexible and grow in bundles of five. On exposed sites, high winds sometimes tear off flakes of weathered bark from the trunk, revealing the deep, red-brown surface beneath.

PISTACHIO / *Pistacia vera*

With their pleasant, mild flavor, the nuts of the pistachio tree have been considered a delicacy since ancient times and the trees have been extensively cultivated. *Pistacia vera* is a small deciduous species with thick, gray leaves that turn a brilliant yellow in the fall. The wood is used for carving and furniture, and all parts of the tree have contributed to various folk-medicine remedies. Pistachio nuts grow in clusters like grapes and are encased in an outer skin or hull. When they ripen, the hull turns rosy and the shell splits, indicating the nut is ready to harvest. Nuts are mostly eaten from the shell, but are also used in candy, baked goods, and ice cream.

Size: Male grows to about 30 feet (9 m), while nut-bearing female is somewhat shorter

Range: Middle East and central Asia; long cultivated in Mediterranean region and more recently in U.S.

LOMBARDY POPLAR / *Populus nigra var. italica*

Populus nigra is generally recognized as the best tree to use for planting in rows closely spaced together, or line planting. The most widely known variety is "Italica"—the Lombardy poplar, used since the 1700s to create magnificent avenues. The tall, columnar shape and sharply ascending branches of the fast-growing Lombardy poplar make it easy to recognize from a distance. The leaves are triangular to almost diamond-shaped and turn golden in the fall. The tree is very susceptible to a canker disease that causes branches to die from the top down and generally kills the tree in twenty-five to thirty years.

Size: Grows 80 to 100 feet (24 to 30 m) tall, with spread of as little as 10 feet (3 m) and diameter of less than 3 feet (1 m)

Range: Native to Europe; planted in U.S. and Canada

YELLOW-POPLAR / *Liriodendron tulipifera*

The yellow-poplar is one of the tallest of all trees in eastern North America. At ten to twenty years old, it begins to bear fragrant tulip-shaped flowers, sometimes hidden from view by the leaves, which open first. The flowers are a light yellow-green at the edges and are crossed with a deep-orange band. They last two to six weeks. The four-lobed leaves are light green as they unfold in spring, shiny, deep green in summer, and golden-yellow in autumn. The leaves are also notched at the tip, giving the appearance of having been clipped. The yellow-poplar is valued as a tree that attracts honeybees to its flowers, and its wood is made into a wide variety of products, including furniture parts, plywood, and pulp.

Size: Grows to average height of 150 feet (46 m), with diameter of 5 feet (1.5 m); on best sites, may be over 200 feet tall (60 m) with diameter of 12 feet (4 m)

Range: Eastern U.S.

Other common names: Tuliptree, tulip poplar

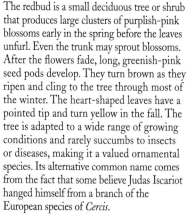

REDBUD / *Cercis canadensis*

Size: Occasionally reaches height of 50 feet (15 m), but generally considerably shorter

Range: Eastern U.S.; population also exists in northeast Mexico

Other common names: Judas tree

The redbud is a small deciduous tree or shrub that produces large clusters of purplish-pink blossoms early in the spring before the leaves unfurl. Even the trunk may sprout blossoms. After the flowers fade, long, greenish-pink seed pods develop. They turn brown as they ripen and cling to the tree through most of the winter. The heart-shaped leaves have a pointed tip and turn yellow in the fall. The tree is adapted to a wide range of growing conditions and rarely succumbs to insects or diseases, making it a valued ornamental species. Its alternative common name comes from the fact that some believe Judas Iscariot hanged himself from a branch of the European species of *Cercis*.

EASTERN REDCEDAR / *Juniperus virginiana*

A small coniferous tree that is valued for its fragrant and beautiful reddish wood, eastern redcedar is used to make cedar chests and closets, where the wood's odor acts as a moth repellent. It is a hardy tree that can withstand the extremes of drought, heat, and cold better than any other North American conifer, and is among the best trees for protecting soils from wind erosion. Eastern redcedar has rounded, purplish cones that look like juicy berries. Branchlets are covered by closely overlapping dark-green scales and new foliage near the tips is pointed and prickly. The tree provides good nesting and roosting cover for many species of birds.

Size: Generally 40 to 50 feet (12 to 15 m) tall, but on good sites may reach 115 feet (35 m)

Range: Eastern half of U.S. north to southern Canada

Other common names: Savin

COAST REDWOOD / *Sequoia sempervirens*

Size: Typically 200 to 330 feet (60 to 100 m) tall, with diameter of 10 to 16 feet (3 to 5 m)

Range: U.S. Pacific coast from southern Oregon to central California

Other common names: California redwood

The magnificent coast redwood thrives on the humidity of the Pacific coast, soaking up the fogs. The world's tallest tree, it often forms pure stands of awe-inspiring grandeur. The trunks rise from massively buttressed bases, sometimes reaching as high as forty-story buildings. The coast redwood is also among the world's oldest trees, with individuals living as long as two or three millennia. The wood is valuable for outdoor use because of its natural decay-resistance, while the burls it produces are prized for making beautiful turned products as well as veneer. Much of the old-growth coast-redwood forests are protected in national and state parks.

DAWN REDWOOD / *Metasequoia glyptostroboides*

Related to the stately coast redwood of California, this Chinese conifer has a romantic history. It was first discovered by scientists in fossilized form in Japan and was thought to be extinct. Shortly afterward, a few living trees were discovered in one location in central China. Seeds collected from these trees were soon germinated in the United States and Britain and planted around the world. Wild members of the species have since been found growing in remote mountain areas of three provinces in China. It is believed the species may have been the primary conifer of northern forests of about a hundred million years ago. The remarkably soft deciduous needles are a bright pale green in the spring and turn a coppery pink in the fall.

Size: Grows 100 feet (30 m) tall

Range: Native to only three provinces of central China

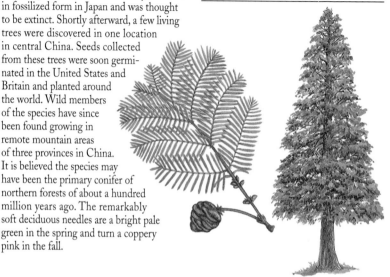

RUSSIAN-OLIVE / *Elaeagnus angustifolia*

Size: Grows to height of about 20 feet (6 m)

Range: Natural range extends from southern Europe to western Asia; now also grown in central and western U.S.

Originally native to southern Europe and central Asia, this small deciduous tree was brought to North America in colonial times. It was cultivated as an ornamental tree and was a favorite choice for windbreaks in the prairies because of its dense branches and drought resistance. In the central and western United States, it has now established itself in the wild and is so hardy that in some places it is usurping the habitat of larger native trees. The tree can be identified by the silvery scales that cover both the underside of the slender leaves and the small, egg-shaped fruits.

SASSAFRAS / *Sassafras albidum*

The leaves, twigs, bark, and roots of the deciduous sassafras tree give off a distinct fragrance when bruised. The twigs are a bright yellow-green and the leaves form in three distinct shapes: entire (smooth-edged, with no "teeth"), mitten-shaped, and three-lobed. The tree's short, stout branches extend from the trunk horizontally and turn upward like the arms of a candelabra. In the spring, just as the leaves unfurl, the sassafras bears clusters of fragrant yellow blossoms. In the autumn, the outer leaves become orange and red, while the leaves closer to the trunk turn yellow, creating the appearance of an inner glow. Early settlers made sassafras tea by boiling the root bark.

Size: Varies from shrub to tree, but can reach height of 100 feet (30 m)

Range: Eastern U.S. and extreme southern Canada

GIANT SEQUOIA / *Sequoiadendron giganteum*

Size: Grows to height of 200 to 350 feet (60 to 105 m), occasionally taller; diameter of 10 to 20 feet (3 to 6 m)

Range: Western slopes of Sierra Nevada in central California

Other common names: Bigtree

The giant sequoia is a true giant among trees; somewhat shorter than its cousin the coast redwood, it is more massive. A single tree can weigh several thousand tons. The buttressed base of this cone-shaped conifer can stretch fifty feet (15 m) in diameter and the bark may be twenty-four inches (60 cm) thick. Like the coast redwood, the giant sequoia has great longevity, with individuals living as long as three thousand years. This awesome tree is also quite rare—found only in about seventy-five groves on the western slopes of California's Sierra Nevada. Most of the groves are now protected from logging.

AMERICAN SMOKETREE / *Cotinus obovatus*

Colorful foliage and delicate flowers make the shrublike American smoketree a popular ornamental species. The rounded leaves emerge bronze-pink in the spring, turn dark green in the summer, and change to various shades of red and orange in the fall, making it a popular cultivar. The many tiny flowers are borne in clusters five to six inches (12 to 15 cm) long until autumn, resembling a cloud of smoke. When cut, the twigs exude a gummy, strong-smelling sap.

Size: Can grow as high as 35 feet (10.5 m)

Range: Sporadically through south-central U.S. states, including Texas, southern Appalachians, Arkansas, Missouri, and Tennessee

Other common names: Smoke bush, wig tree

STAGHORN SUMAC / *Rhus typhina*

Size: Ranges in height from 20 to 50 feet (6 to 15 m)

Range: Northeastern U.S. and southeastern Canada

Other common names: Velvet sumac

The handsome, fernlike foliage of the staghorn sumac is composed of leaves that have eleven to thirty leaflets growing from reddish, fuzzy stalks. The leaves turn bright red or orange in winter. The small red fruits are covered with reddish hairs and sit erect at the tip of twigs in dense, crimson clusters. The fruits remain on the tree throughout most of the winter and are a source of food for many species of birds. In winter, the spreading branches of the staghorn sumac look like the antlers of a stag, hence the name. The wood is light, brittle, and beautifully grained.

SYCAMORE / *Platanus occidentalis*

The sycamore is one of the largest trees of the eastern deciduous forests and was once used by Native Americans for dugout canoes. It thrives in lowlands and in abandoned fields and is popular as a shade tree. The sycamore is most notable for its light-colored flaking bark. With three to five lobes, the leaves can measure as much as eight inches (20 cm) across. Both the flowers and the fruit grow in hanging globular clusters. When a fruit cluster breaks up, each seed is carried off in the wind, thanks to a tuft of dark hairs. One of the common names refers to the fact that the woody fruit of the sycamore was used to make buttons in frontier times.

Size: Up to 115 feet (35 m) tall, with diameter of up to 10 feet (3 m)

Range: Eastern U.S. as far south as Georgia

Other common names: American planetree, buttonwood

TANOAK / *Lithocarpus densiflorus*

Size: Generally 50 to 90 feet (15 to 28 m) tall, but height of 130 feet (40 m) not uncommon

Range: Limited to California and Oregon on U.S. west coast

Other common names: Tanbark oak

Once mistakenly thought to be an oak because of the acorns it bears, the tanoak is an evergreen with leathery, oblong leaves and flowers that resemble those of a chestnut tree. It is placed in a separate genus, but is closely related to oak and chestnut; all three belong to the beech family, Fagaceae. The appearance of the tanoak varies widely, depending on growing conditions. In dense coniferous forests, its narrow crown and ascending branches give it a stately look. In open areas, the trunk is short and thick and splits into several large branches to create a broad crown. The native people of the northern California coast depended on the large, bitter acorns for food. The high oil content made them a popular ingredient in soup, bread, and other foods.

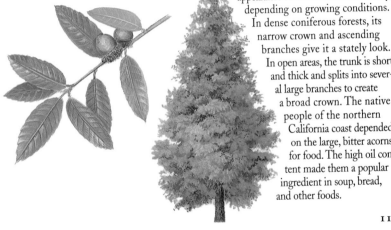

BLACK TUPELO / Nyssa sylvatica

A relatively unremarkable-looking deciduous tree, the black tupelo tends to go unnoticed—until the fall. Then, it puts on one of the best shows of any tree, turning a uniform yellow, orange, red, or purple, or displaying a mixture of colors at once. The black tupelo produces unobtrusive greenish flowers that are a favorite with honeybees. Male and female flowers grow primarily on separate trees, but a few flowers of the opposite sex can appear on the same tree. As a result, some trees yield much more abundant fruit than others.

Size: Grows 120 feet (36 m) tall, with diameter of up to 4 feet (1.2 m)

Range: Throughout eastern U.S. from New England south to Florida

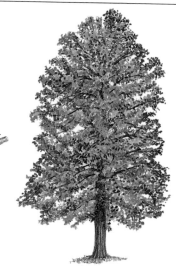

BLACK WALNUT / Juglans nigra

Size: From 50 to 75 feet (15 to 23 m) tall

Range: Throughout eastern North America with scatterings farther west

A deciduous tree with a straight trunk and feathery leaves, the European black walnut tree has been valued for its nuts as far back as Roman times. In North America, most stands of the biggest black walnut trees between the Appalachian Mountains and the Mississippi were felled by the end of the nineteenth century to make way for farmland. Today the beautifully grained brown wood is often used in solid stock for cabinetmaking. This attractive and useful tree has a nasty side: Older trees exude a poisonous substance, called juglone, from their roots, killing neighboring trees. For this reason, the tree generally grows in pure stands. A black walnut tree in your yard can be a menace to other trees and plants.

BABYLON WEEPING WILLOW / *Salix babylonica*

Planted in parks and gardens in many warmer parts of the world, the Babylon weeping willow is widely considered the most beautiful of all the weeping willows. A fast-growing species with long, pendulous branches that may reach down to the ground, the tree thrives in moist soil and can often be seen alongside streams and ponds. The graceful branches move in the slightest breeze, but are brittle and easily broken by high winds or ice storms. Young branches are yellow-green in color and thickly set with narrow, lancelike leaves. A hybrid of the tree has been developed that is better suited to winter climates.

Size: Grows 30 to 50 feet (9 to 15 m) tall, with short, thick trunk 3 to 5 feet (1 to 1.5 m) in diameter

Range: Native to Persia, but now widely planted throughout world

BLACK WILLOW / *Salix nigra*

The black willow is a short-lived, deciduous tree with a trunk that usually leans and is often divided. The bark is thick and deeply furrowed; the leaves are long and narrow. The tree is often found with its trunk leaning out over the water along rivers and streams. The wood of *Salix nigra* was once used extensively for artificial limbs because it is lightweight, holds its shape well, and doesn't splinter easily. During colonial times, the wood served as a source of charcoal in gunpowder. Today it is used for furniture, toys, baskets, and pulpwood.

Size: Tree or shrub on average 65 feet (20 m) tall, with trunk 16 inches (40 cm) in diameter; crown broad and open, with stout branches

Range: Throughout eastern U.S. and adjacent parts of Canada and Mexico

Other common names: Swamp willow

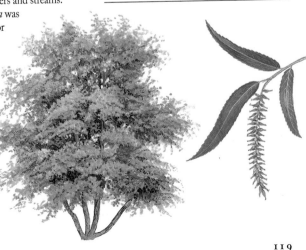

Tropical

The two key controlling factors of temperature and available moisture that dictate the type of forests in temperate regions also help orchestrate diversity in the tropics. The major difference, however, is that in tropical forests temperature plays less of a deciding role than the amount and seasonality of rainfall.

The risk of frost within the tropics is negligible, except at higher elevations, but where frost does occur occasionally the forests are remarkably similar to those found in the temperate zone. In rare instances, even species of conifers adapted to boreal conditions are found in the upland tropical biome. For example, the eastern white pine (*Pinus strobus*), a major constituent of the forests of eastern Canada, grows sparingly in the highlands of Guatemala. Similarly, species of Araucariaceae, a primitive family of southern-hemisphere conifers, are abundant enough in the Andes of northern Chile and southwestern Brazil to be an important timber resource. But these temperature-altered forests are few and far between within the tropical zone.

On the surface, it would seem that since moisture rather than temperature presents the controlling environmental factor in the tropics, the plant kingdom would be obliged to address it with a totally unique battery of adaptive survival techniques, but this is not the case. Viewed closely, the plant kingdom's bag of tricks turns out

to be essentially the same for all environments. The difference rests in how and when the various adaptive techniques are employed. Just as temperate, deciduous angiosperms such as maple (*Acer*), ash (*Fraxinus*), and elm (*Ulmus*) shed their leaves because frigid winter temperatures interrupt their ability to metabolize, prolonged drought in the tropics can trigger dormancy and leaf-shedding. These extremely harsh, monsoonal conditions, where the entire year's precipitation falls during a brief rainy season, are less universal in the tropics than winter is in the temperate zone, but they do exist in south-central Africa and parts of Southeast Asia.

Just as the evergreen conifers manage to handle the desiccating conditions of frigid winter air because their needles have a more limited surface area, many tropical, broad-leaved angiosperms have more succulent foliage than their temperate counterparts. Regardless of what seasonal conditions restrict the availability of moisture, the key to a tree's survival is to retain as much of it as possible during times of scarcity. Succulent foliage helps to achieve this objective in all but the harshest and most arid of tropical forests, allowing the vast majority of tropical tree species to remain evergreen. While the annual rate of growth is not always uniform in the tropical biome, it is generally continuous.

Where moisture is available in at least adequate amounts, the tropics provide a kinder and gentler environment for plant growth and, as a result, this zone tends to host a greater number of arboreal species. While the rain-forest biome represents the ultimate in diversity, even the less ideal conditions of the tropical biome allow many species to attain tree size when the families and genera to which they belong are represented only by herbs and shrubs in the forests of the temperate zone.

Deciduous trees are found not only in temperate regions but also in the tropics, where the lush vegetation can be adversely affected by drought.

ALBIZZIA / *Albizia lebbek*

Size: Can attain height of 100 feet (30 m), with wide-spreading crown

Range: Native to tropical and subtropical Asia, East Africa, and Australia, but introduced and cultivated all over world in subtropical and tropical regions

Other common names: Women's tongue tree, rattle pod, East Indian walnut

This handsome and hardy tree is fast growing and has a multitude of practical uses. Its leaves and young twigs make good livestock fodder, while the bark, leaves, and seeds are used in herbal medicines, soap-making, and tannin production. Beekeepers like albizzia for the light-colored honey produced from its nectar. The leaves have four to ten pairs of leaflets per leaf. The abundant and fluffy flowers are fragrant and yellow-green and develop into large, flat papery pods up to twelve inches (30 cm) long. The noise of the pods shaking in the wind makes a rattling sound that is the source of two of the tree's common names.

ALLSPICE / *Pimenta diocia*

This is a small evergreen tree, the unripe berries of which provide the seasoning that bears its name—so called because it combines the flavors of cloves, nutmeg, and cinnamon, making it one of the most desirable of all aromatic and pungent spices for more than three hundred years. Spanish explorers thought the fruit resembled black pepper-corns and gave it the name *pimienta*. The tree has large, shiny, oblong leaves with prominent veins underneath and they emit a clovelike odor when crushed. The fruits are small and dark blue and grow in clusters. Berries are gath-ered when mature but still green because the fully ripened fruit loses much of its aromatic qualities.

Size: Grows to height of 35 feet (11 m) with numerous branches and dense foliage

Range: Native to Caribbean Islands; Jamaica most important producer

AVOCADO / *Persea americana*

Size: Grows to height of 60 feet (18 m)

Range: Central America

An evergreen tree with long, leathery leaves and tiny, unobtrusive flowers, the avocado is distinguished from other members of its genus by its large edible fruit. There are two common wild varieties of avocado. The Mexican version is identified by the thin, smooth skin of its fruit and the anise scent given off by its leaves when crushed. The Guatemalan variety produces fruit with a thicker, more fibrous skin. The fruit of the avocado can vary in shape from almost spher-ical to pear-shaped and can weigh as much as two pounds (1 kg). Its flesh is creamy and rich in oil and vitamins.

BOTTLEBRUSH / *Callistemon*

All the members of the genus *Callistemon* are native to Australia. They are evergreen trees with small, pointy leaves known for the unusual flowers that are the source of the tree's name. Growing in long clusters along the branchlets, the flowers have small petals, but exceptionally long stamens, which give the clusters a bristly look. Even odder, the young branchlets simply keep growing out from the end of the cluster, so the branches end up being encased with the blooms—either yellow-green or scarlet, depending on the species. The resulting display makes the bottlebrush tree a popular choice for tropical gardens.

Size: Up to 30 feet (9 m) in height

Range: Australia

BREADFRUIT / *Artocarpus altilis*

Size: Up to 100 feet (30 m) tall, with thick, straight trunk

Range: Native to South Pacific, but cultivated or naturalized throughout all humid tropics

Other common names: Breadnut (seeded variety)

This fast-growing tree yields large, edible fruit and is a popular home garden tree in many tropical parts of the world. The fruit is rounded, with a rough skin that turns yellowish brown when ripe. It is harvested as a starch vegetable when still green and is fermented or boiled and dried for use in bread-making. The breadfruit is associated with the famous mutiny on the *Bounty* in 1787. Captain Bligh was en route to deliver a thousand breadfruit plants from Tahiti to the West Indies in an attempt to transplant this useful fruit when the crew rose against him. Bligh was nicknamed "Breadfruit Bligh."

CALABASH / *Crescentia cujete*

A small evergreen tree, the calabash produces peculiar flowers and fruits. The bell-shaped flowers are yellow or purple and spring in clusters straight from the trunk or larger branches. The blooms open at night, giving off an unpleasant odor. The melon-shaped fruits start out green and then turn reddish brown. They are used as water gourds after the peel and the seeds have been removed and the hard shell polished.

The green fruit can be tied while still on the tree to force it to grow into other shapes convenient as containers. Perhaps the most famous use of the calabash is for tobacco pipes, such as the one identified with Sherlock Holmes.

Size: Grows to maximum height of 40 feet (12 m)

Range: Tropical areas of Caribbean, Central America, and central and southern Africa

Other common names: Gourd tree

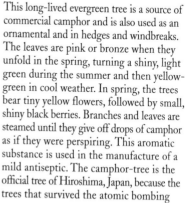

CAMPHOR-TREE / *Cinnamomum camphora*

Size: From 30 to 50 feet (9 to 15 m) tall, with broadly spreading crown; individuals as tall as 82 feet (25 m) recorded

Range: Native to Asia, but cultivated or naturalized in Australia and extreme southern U.S.

This long-lived evergreen tree is a source of commercial camphor and is also used as an ornamental and in hedges and windbreaks. The leaves are pink or bronze when they unfold in the spring, turning a shiny, light green during the summer and then yellow-green in cool weather. In spring, the trees bear tiny yellow flowers, followed by small, shiny black berries. Branches and leaves are steamed until they give off drops of camphor as if they were perspiring. This aromatic substance is used in the manufacture of a mild antiseptic. The camphor-tree is the official tree of Hiroshima, Japan, because the trees that survived the atomic bombing recovered quickly, providing a source of hope and strength to the citizens there.

CANNONBALL-TREE / *Couroupita guianensis*

A huge deciduous tree, the cannonball is named for the round woody fruit that hangs from its dangling branches. The six- to eight-inch (15- to 20-cm) -long fruits mature on the tree for about eighteen months before they fall to the ground, breaking open and emitting an unpleasant odor. The fragrant, orchidlike flowers are almost as unusual. About five inches (12 cm) across, with waxy petals, yellowish on the outside and crimson inside, they push their way out directly from the bark of the branch, independent of the long leaves growing at the end of the branchlets.

Size: Grows to maximum height of 80 feet (24 m)

Range: Central America, parts of Caribbean, and northern South America

CARAMBOLA / *Averrhoa carambola*

Size: Rarely more than 30 feet (9 m) in height, with spread of roughly 20 feet (6 m)

Range: Native to Southeast Asia, but cultivated or naturalized throughout most of tropical and warm subtropical areas of world

Other common names: Star fruit

The carambola is a slow-growing evergreen tree that produces an edible fruit. The fruit is star-shaped in cross-section, yellow to orange when ripe, with an unusual translucent, smooth, and waxy skin. It contains twelve thin, flat seeds. The flavor varies from sour to sweet. The fruit is generally consumed fresh in salads and desserts, but some is processed into jellies and tarts. Flowers are pink to purplish and borne in clusters. They are very short-lived, blooming during the daytime and wilting during the night of the same day. Trade in carambola is expanding world-wide as people become more familiar with the unique shape and taste of its fruit.

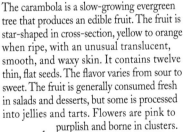

CASHEW / *Anacardium occidentale*

The spreading branches of this small evergreen are often so twisted that they reach the ground. The leaves are blue-green and leathery and the small, pinkish blossoms are fragrant. The cashew tree is cultivated for its nut, which is enclosed in a hard, kidney-shaped shell. The shell contains an oil that makes human skin blister, so the nuts must be roasted before the kernel can be removed. The nut grows out of the end of the pear-shaped "cashew fruit," which is also edible. It is, in fact, not a fruit, but an enlargement of the stalk behind the nut or true fruit.

Size: Up to 45 feet (14 m) tall

Range: East coast of Brazil

SPANISH-CEDAR / *Cedrela odorata*

Size: As tall as 100 to 130 feet (30 to 40 m)

Range: Moist tropical and subtropical forests from Mexico to South America; planted in parts of Africa

Other common names: Cedro hembra, cigar-box cedar

The pink or reddish wood of the Spanish-cedar contains an insect-repelling resin, the fragrance of which resembles the aroma of the true cedars (*Cedrus*), making it a popular choice for household furniture to store clothing. It is also used to make cigar boxes and humidors because it imparts a special flavor to tobacco. The wood is naturally termite- and rot-resistant and is therefore suitable for exterior construction. The fruit is a large woody capsule that ripens, splits, and sheds winged seeds while still attached to the tree. Spanish-cedar is quite exacting in its site requirements, preferring well-drained and well-aerated soils. Despite the tree's common name, it is not a conifer. Its numbers are declining because of overharvesting.

CHERIMOYA / *Annona cherimola*

This small deciduous tree is greatly prized for its fruits, which have been called one of the most exquisite in the world. The fruits vary in shape from spherical to conical and typically weigh from four to six pounds (2 to 3 kg). The skin can be either smooth or bumpy. The white flesh has a custardlike texture that melts in the mouth and a flavor somewhere between banana and pineapple. The fruits are preceded by small fragrant flowers. Trees of the genus Annona were cultivated as long ago as 2500 B.C.

Size: Grows to height of 25 to 30 feet (7 to 9 m)

Range: Mountain valleys of Ecuador and Peru

CINNAMON / *Cinnamomum verum*

Size: Up to 65 feet (20 m) tall in wild, but continuous harvesting produces dense bushy plant no more than 10 feet (3 m) tall

Range: Sri Lanka and west coast of India

The evergreen trees that produce the popular cinnamon spice are rarely allowed to attain their natural height under cultivation. Every two years young shoots are cut off close to the ground and the bark—which peels off easily if the cutting is done in the rainy season—is removed in two long strips. The outer skin is scraped off and the strips are slowly dried into what are called "quills," which curl and turn light brown. The quills are then cut to short lengths and sold as cinnamon sticks. Ground cinnamon is used in curry powders and for flavoring candy and baked goods.

DRAGONTREE / *Dracaena draco*

Native to the Canary Islands, the dragontree is one of only a few trees that belong to the lily family. It has spearlike leaves up to twenty-four inches (60 cm) long that bristle from the end of the branches.

The tree produces tiny greenish flowers and orange berries, and owes its name to the thick red sap yielded by the older trees, thought to look like dragon's blood. Dragontrees live to a great age; one currently living is thought to be more than two thousand years old.

Size: Can grow to 60 feet (18 m) or more

Range: Canary Islands

COMMON FIG / *Ficus carica*

Size: Grows as small shrub or tree up to 30 feet (9 m) high, with trunk rarely larger than 7 inches (18 cm) in diameter

Range: Probably native to western Asia; widespread in warm temperate and subtropical regions

Fig trees have been cultivated for their fruit for thousands of years. Seed size ranges from large to minute and the numbers vary from thirty to sixteen hundred per fruit, giving some figs a crunchy texture. The tender skin of fresh figs makes them difficult to transport and they are only consumed close to where they are grown. Figs are also eaten dried, preserved, or canned. The latex of unripe fruits and branches may be severely irritating to the skin and is an occupational hazard for the people who harvest figs.

FLAMBOYANT TREE / Delonix regia (Poinciana) Madagascar

This tree richly deserves its name. It is one of the showiest flowering trees of the tropics. In early spring, dense clusters of brilliant orange and scarlet flowers make the tree look like it has suddenly caught fire, earning it the alternate common name of "flame tree." The display continues until late summer. A broadly spreading tree, it has delicate fernlike leaves that are deciduous for a short season. The fruits are brown pods up to fifteen inches (38 cm) long, the seeds of which are sometimes used as beads. The flamboyant tree is planted as an ornamental in warm climates around the world.

Size: Up to 50 feet (15 m) tall

Range: Native to Madagascar, but now grown in tropical regions worldwide

Other common names: Royal poinciana, flame tree

GUAVA / Psidium guajava

Size: Usually shrub, but in areas with high moisture grows 20 to 30 feet (6 to 9 m) tall with diameter of 12 inches (30 cm) or more

Range: Native to American tropics, but thrives in many tropical and subtropical regions

Other common names: Guajaba

The guava tree grows and produces fruit under poor soil conditions, making it one of the least demanding of all tropical fruit trees. The flowers create abundant seeds that remain viable for a long time, resulting in a tree that spreads so easily it has become a pest in some regions. Young green twigs are square in shape and the branches are flexible, rarely broken by strong winds. The yellow fruits are roundish, about the size of an egg, and have a distinctive, musky flavor. The ripe flesh may be pink, white, or yellow and is embedded with hard seeds. The pulp has a grainy texture like that of a pear.

JACARANDA / *Jacaranda mimosifolia*

The jacaranda is a low-branching deciduous tree with soft, feathery fernlike leaves. In the early spring, the jacaranda is covered with lovely purple-blue, bell-shaped flowers that carpet the ground as they fall. Some varieties have white blooms. The flat, round seed pods that follow enclose numerous thin-winged seeds. The jacaranda is a native of Brazil, but is popular as a street tree in places as far away as Australia and South Africa. Pretoria, awash with purple in the spring, likes to call itself the jacaranda capital.

Size: Grows to about 30 feet (9 m)

Range: Native to Brazil, but grows commonly elsewhere in South America as well as in Central America and Mexico

Other common names: Fern tree

KAPOKTREE / *Ceiba pentandra*

Size: Grows to 200 feet (60 m) or more with broadly spreading crown of up to 165 feet (50 m); trunk diameter above buttresses may be 10 feet (3 m)

Range: Native to Africa, South America, tropical Asia

Other common names: Ceiba, silk-cotton

The branches of the massive kapoktree are very thick next to the trunk, but taper outward, giving the tree an almost triangular appearance. The tree blooms every two years into tassel-like flowers, producing a capsule-like fruit four to ten inches (10 to 25 cm) long. Cottony hairs surround the seeds inside the capsule. These hairs are cylindrical and contain cells that are full of air and impermeable to moisture, making kapok a useful material for flotation devices, upholstery, and insulation against sound and heat. The tree was widely cultivated in the tropics but kapok has now been largely replaced by synthetic materials.

KAURI / *Agathis australis*

Size: Grows to height of 150 feet (45 m) and to diameter of up to 9 feet (3 m)

Range: *Agathis australis* is native to northern New Zealand; similar *A. robusta* grows in Australia

Other common names: Kauri pine

The kauri of New Zealand belongs to a family of conifers found only in the southern hemisphere. For the first period of its life, the tree has an unremarkable conical shape. After about fifty years, however, it begins to take on adult proportions as its lower branches are shed and the upper ones spread outward. Mature trees dominate the forest, with massive trunks often free of branches up to a height of more than fifty feet (15 m) and an immense crown that dwarfs everything around it. The kauri has the unusual characteristic of constantly shedding its bark in flakes, which pile up in mounds as deep as five feet (1.5 m) around the base of the tree.

LIGNUMVITAE / *Guaiacum officinale*

The name lignumvitae means "wood of life," a reference to the tree's exaggerated reputation in late medieval times as a source of medication for many serious diseases—a reputation that made the tree a very valuable commodity. It was not until several hundred years later that these claims were finally debunked. Lignumvitae is a slow-growing evergreen that produces the heaviest wood of any tree in the world—so dense that it actually sinks in water. It contains an oily resin that gives it self-lubricating properties, making it suitable for products such as underwater bearings.

Size: Grows from 40 to 65 feet (12 to 20 m) tall; trunk almost always crooked

Range: Caribbean region

LYCHEE / *Litchi chinensis*

A small, dense evergreen, the lychee has glossy leaves and a broad top. The small greenish-yellow flowers—a favorite of honeybees—have no petals. The tree is cultivated in warm regions of Asia for the small globular fruit that hangs from the tree in loose clusters. The leathery skin of the fruit is covered with small knobs and is reddish when ripe. Fresh, the lychee fruit has the texture of grapes and a perfumy, slightly acidic taste. Dried, it is sold as lychee nuts. The lychee tree can live for many centuries, and a few individuals are thought to be more than a thousand years old.

Size: Up to 40 feet tall (12 m), with trunk up to 10 feet (3 m) in diameter

Range: Native to China and Philippines

Other common names: Litchi, litchee, leechee

MANGO / *Mangifera indica*

Size: Height ranges from 25 to 80 feet (7.5 to 25 m)

Range: Native to Burma, India, and parts of Far East; also widely grown in almost every tropical country as well as in many subtropical regions

Mango trees have been cultivated in India for thousands of years. The fruit is prominent in Hindu mythology and is mentioned in numerous ancient Sanskrit poems. The fruit varies widely in size, shape, and color, but the pulp is usually orange and very juicy and surrounds a large, flattened seed. In the best mangoes, the pulp is entirely free of fibers and boasts a smooth, melting texture. In inferior fruits, the pulp can be stringy, with a taste reminiscent of turpentine. Narrow, dark-green leaves form a dense mass of foliage that casts heavy shade and provides a favorable habitat for mosquitoes.

NUTMEG / *Myristica fragrans*

Beginning in the sixteenth century, the Portuguese and then the Dutch vied to control the Moluccas, or Spice Islands, in the Far East because of their native nutmeg trees. The trees were prized for their seeds, from which nutmeg powder is produced. The seeds are contained in a yellow fruit resembling an apricot that splits open when ripe. Each seed is surrounded by a red covering, or aril, that is used as another spice, mace. The tree is a large evergreen with brownish oval leaves and inconspicuous yellow flowers.

Size: Grows about 70 feet (21 m) high

Range: Native to the Moluccas, formerly called Spice Islands, south of Philippines, but now cultivated in tropical places outside its native islands

SWEET ORANGE / *Citrus sinensis*

Size: Grows about 25 feet (7.5 m) tall

Range: Native to southern China and Southeast Asia, but now grown worldwide in tropical and subtropical regions

The sweet orange is part of a genus of small, broadleaf evergreen trees originating in China and Southeast Asia. It produces the fruit that we know simply as "oranges," as opposed to the "sour oranges" produced by its close cousin. Like all members of the genus, it has dark shiny leaves containing translucent glands that emit a strong aroma when crushed. The white flowers are also fragrant. The sweet orange was first brought to the Americas by Columbus. It is now grown commercially throughout the southern United States, from California to Florida.

ROYAL PALM / *Roystonea regia*

Elegant, stately, and highly ornamental, the royal palm is known for its striking, pale-gray trunk, which resembles a cathedral pillar molded from concrete. The graceful, feathery leaves arch in all directions from a green cylinder of leaf sheaths at the top of the trunk, giving the crown a very round shape. The leaves are about ten feet (3 m) long, composed of bright green leaflets. Branched violet flowers develop in clusters and produce oval and dark-colored fruit. The tree's Latin name comes from General Roy Stone, a U.S. army engineer who served in the Caribbean in the early 1900s.

Size: Grows 50 to 75 feet (15 to 23 m) tall

Range: Native to Caribbean; planted in U.S. and elsewhere in tropical and subtropical regions

Other common names: Cuban royal palm

PAPAYA / *Carica papaya*

Size: Can grow to height of 25 feet (7.5 m)

Range: Native to tropical America, but widely planted throughout tropics

The papaya tree is an extremely fast-growing, but short-lived tree that has no branches. The evergreen leaves grow on stout, hollow stems from the top of the trunk and they are palm-shaped with pointed lobes. New leaves form constantly and old leaves die and fall off. The papaya tree will bear fruit after just one year of growth, but after three or four years the tree's productivity declines. The fruit has a thick, yellowish-green skin and a sweet, pink or orange flesh containing many dark seeds. The milky sap of stems and young fruit contains papain, an enzyme that breaks down protein and is used as a meat tenderizer.

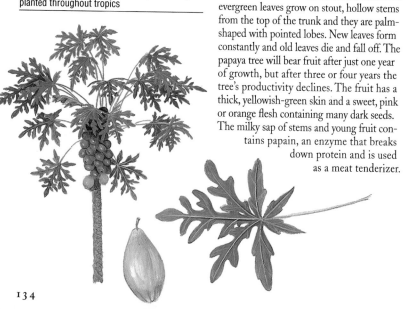

POMEGRANATE / *Punica granatum*

Ancient paintings and carvings reveal that the pomegranate has been cultivated for at least five thousand years. It is a spreading shrub or small tree with narrow, glossy, deciduous leaves. The fruit, about the size of an orange, contains a sweet, juicy, reddish pulp filled with numerous small seeds. The pulp is edible and is used for syrups and jams. The tree is cultivated as much for its flowers as for its fruit. They can be up to four inches (10 cm) across, range in color from soft yellow to bright orange or red, and have a single or double row of petals.

Size: Grows about 20 feet (6 m) tall

Range: Native from Mediterranean to Himalayas

SANDALWOOD / *Santalum album*

Size: Grows to 40 feet (12 m) in height

Range: India and Southeast Asia

Sandalwood oil was used in India as a perfume as long ago as 500 B.C. The tree that is its source is a small evergreen with oval leaves and plentiful small flowers that start out yellowish and then turn red. The wood has no scent when it is first cut, but a distinctive aroma emerges as the wood dries. Traditionally the felled trees were allowed to lie in the forest for several months and only trimmed and sawn once the useless sapwood had been eaten away by ants. Sandalwood plays an important role in Indian rituals. A paste of the wood is smeared on religious statues. Sandalwood is also burned as incense and often used for funeral pyres.

SAPODILLA / *Manilkara zapota*

The sapodilla is an evergreen with branches that often extend from the trunk horizontally and are tough and pliable, making them more resistant to hurricanes than many other tropical fruit trees. The leaves are thick, stiff, and shiny. The sapodilla tree produces a round fruit with brownish, rough skin. When immature, the fruit contains tannins and a milky latex and is inedible. When ripe, however, the soft, sweet pulp is yellowish brown and filled with large, black seeds. It has an attractive flavor, rather like brown sugar. Latex is also produced beneath the bark. Incisions are made to allow the latex to flow out and it is collected and boiled to make chicle, an important ingredient in chewing gum.

Size: Reaches height of 50 to 100 feet (15 to 30 m) with dense rounded or conical crown

Range: Native to Mexico and Central America

SAUSAGE TREE / *Kigelia pinnata*

Size: Reaches height of 50 feet (15 m)

Range: Africa

The sausage tree is so named for its bizarre two-foot (60-cm) -long fruits, one of the oddest-looking of any tropical tree. The fruit is preceded by flowers almost as peculiar. The large, trumpet-shaped brownish red blooms grow on dangling stalks that turn up at the end so the nectar doesn't spill out. Both the flowers and fruits are favored by wildlife. The flowers open at night, giving off an unpleasant smell that is attractive to bats, while monkeys and baboons relish both the nectar and the fibrous fruit. The tree itself is a broad-topped evergreen with long, leathery leaves.

SILKY-OAK / *Grevillea robusta*

The silky-oak is a fast-growing evergreen tree with lustrous wood that is highly sought after for cabinetmaking. The tree has a distinctive profile with horizontal branches and green, fernlike leaves that are silvery below. It is magnificent in spring, when the flowers create a dense golden brush that is attractive to birds seeking their nectar. Silky-oak is very adaptable and is frequently found as an ornamental tree in gardens and along streets. It is also used as a shade tree in tea, banana, and coffee plantations around the world.

Size: Grows to 130 feet (40 m)

Range: Native to Australia, but planted as ornamental throughout world

Other common names: Lacewood

TEAK / *Tectona grandis*

Size: From 100 to 130 feet (30 to 40 m) tall with small buttresses at base of trunk

Range: Native to Southeast Asia and widely cultivated in plantations in many tropical regions of world

Teak is one of the most commercially important timber trees in the world. The golden-brown heartwood is hard, heavy, and strong and very resistant to decay. It is remarkable for its lack of movement under changes of moisture and temperature and it is therefore very valuable as decking for boats. Teak wood has a straight, even grain and is also widely used for outdoor furniture. The tree has large eight- to twenty-inch (20- to 50-cm) -long oval-shaped leaves that are shed during the dry season. White or bluish flowers appear, scattered in large panicles, and one inflorescence may have thousands of flowers, with about a hundred opening daily for several weeks.

137

TRAVELER'S-TREE / *Ravenala madagascariensis*

Size: Height at maturity varies from
30 to 80 feet (9 to 24 m)

Range: Native to Madagascar, but widely
planted as ornamental

The huge, oblong leaves of the
traveler's-tree spread out in a
single row from the top of an
unbranched trunk, giving the
overall appearance of a giant
fan. New growth occurs in the
middle of this fan and old leaves
die back at the fan edges. Each
leaf is on a long stalk with a cup-
shaped trough at the base that can
collect almost one quart (1 l) of rain
water. The tree received its name because
thirsty travelers can drink this water in
an emergency. The large flower clusters have
reddish green bracts and creamy white flowers with light blue seeds.

TREE FERN / *Cyathea*

Size: Some species exceed 70 feet (21 m)
in height; others may be less than 10 feet
(3 m) tall

Range: Grows in humid tropical lands; often
cultivated as ornamental in cooler regions,
but must be protected during cold weather

The genus *Cyathea* includes many magnificent species of ferns, all of which have feathery green fronds and resemble palm trees.
The fronds unfurl at the apex of the trunk
and may reach twenty feet (6 m) in length.
Tree ferns have no flowers, fruits, or seeds but
reproduce by means of spores formed on the
underside of the fronds. In most species, the
old fronds and leaf stems eventually die, leaving distinctive scars on the trunk, which are
often arranged in a spiral pattern. These old,
brown fronds form a characteristic skirt
around the top of the trunk. The trunk is
often covered with a dense layer of hairs or
even spines. The leaf buds, or "croziers," may
have a profuse covering
of spines or scales that
gives protection from
frost and fire to some
species of tree ferns. After
the expanded fronds have been
killed, the unharmed croziers can
unfurl and allow the fern grow again.

TREE-OF-HEAVEN/ *Ailanthus altissima*

A deciduous tree, the tree-of-heaven is so aggressive that it is considered a weed in many places. It springs up in vacant lots and along roadsides and even pushes its way up through cracks in the sidewalk. It owes its success to the speed at which seedlings establish a taproot (about three months), the abundance of its seeds, and its ability to spread with root suckers, sending up new shoots as much as fifty feet (15 m) from the original plant. The bark and leaves of the tree-of-heaven even produce a toxin that inhibits the growth of other plants.

Size: Up to 90 feet (27 m) tall

Range: Originally native to China, but naturalized in much of Europe and North America

Other common names: Chinese sumac

AFRICAN TULIP TREE / *Spathodea campanulata*

Size: Commonly 25 to 40 feet (7.5 to 12 m) tall, but can grow to 70 feet (21 m)

Range: Western Africa

Other common names: Fountain tree

A popular ornamental tree in many parts of the tropics, the African tulip tree is a broadleaf evergreen with dark green feathery leaves. It produces dark, claw-shaped buds that exude so much water that the tree is also known as the fountain tree. The buds are followed by large, cup-shaped orange or scarlet flowers that cluster at the end of the branchlets and give off a distinctive scent. The fruit is as much as eight inches (20 cm) long and contains large, silver-colored winged seeds. The African tulip tree is rarely seen outside the tropics because of its sensitivity to frost.

Northern Boreal

The northern boreal forests span the globe in a virtually continuous band across northern Europe, Siberia, and North America. To the north lies the tundra, so inhospitable that it hosts only a few dwarfed forms of woody plants. To the south are the deciduous hardwood forests of the temperate zone, posing an equally formidable barrier.

pockets—usually on poorer soils or at higher elevations—where angiosperms cannot compete. In the boreal forests, conifers still reign supreme and the broad-leaved angiosperms are the intruders, represented by only a few hardy species such as birch (*Betula*) and aspen (*Populus*).

Conifers may be descendants of early trees, but northern boreal forests are relatively young. Much of the terrain, scraped to the bedrock by glaciers that receded only ten thousand years ago, is in the soil-building stage, as lakes become peat bogs and eventually dry land. As a result, an equally slow process of succession is occurring in the species mix. While species with a higher tolerance for saturated soils, such as tamarack (*Larix*), black spruce (*Picea mariana*), and cedar (*Thuja*), colonize the edge of the bogs, pines (*Pinus*) and firs (*Abies*) encroach behind them.

Despite long cold winters and short summers, the boreal regions of the northern hemisphere are characterized by a dense forest of conifers.

Boreal forests are the last major bastion of the conifers that arose early in the course of tree evolution. Conifers do persist elsewhere, but mostly as minor constituents in deciduous forests or in isolated

Boreal forests are a tremendous resource in terms of timber and fiber for paper production and other industrial products. But harsh winter conditions and short growing seasons make for agonizingly slow regeneration.

RED ALDER / *Alnus rubra*

The most common hardwood of the Pacific Northwest, red alder is a rapid-growing, short-lived tree. Because it has comparatively limited commercial value, forest managers have often attempted to eliminate it from coniferous stands. However, with the discovery that the roots of the tree increase nitrogen levels in soil, experiments are being carried out to see if planting red alders will improve conditions for surrounding trees. The wood has an attractive fine grain, making it suitable for furniture. It is also used for making plywood, tissue paper, and writing paper.

Size: On favorable sites, reaches height of 95 to 130 feet (29 to 40 m)

Range: Pacific Coast from California to Alaska, generally within 125 miles (200 km) of ocean and at elevations below 2,500 feet (750 m)

Other common names: Oregon alder, western alder, Pacific Coast alder

AMERICAN MOUNTAIN ASH / *Sorbus americana*

Size: From 40 to 80 feet (12 to 25 m) in height

Range: Eastern Canada and U.S.

The mountain ash is a small deciduous tree with white flowers and large leaves composed of nine to eleven leaflets. The tree's bright-red berries hang on the tree through the autumn as the leaves turn a burnished gold, later providing food to birds such as grosbeaks, grouse, and cedar waxwings. Moose eat the tree's foliage, winter twigs, and fragrant inner bark. In Micmac culture, the inner bark was steeped in water to make a tea for treating stomach pains, while the wood was used for canoe frames and snowshoes. Mountain ash is not a true ash, but is easily confused with the European ash, which was introduced to North America as an ornamental tree, but now often grows wild.

BLACK ASH / *Fraxinus nigra*

This slender deciduous tree thrives in wet conditions, such as in swamps and bogs and on riverbanks and lakeshores, often with its trunk leaning out over the water. The leaves are compound, with a number of opposite pairs of leaves forming a feathery group. Like other ashes, the tree produces an abundance of distinctive winged seeds that are carried long distances by the wind. Both the leaves and seeds are important sources of food for wildlife. The wood, not as strong as that of other ashes, is used for interior trim, cabinets, and veneer.

Size: Reaches height of 60 to 70 feet (18 to 21 m), with diameter of 12 to 24 inches (30 to 60 cm)

Range: Eastern Canada and U.S. from Newfoundland to Manitoba and south to Virginia

PAPER BIRCH / *Betula papyrifera*

Size: Grows to height of 80 to 115 feet (25 to 35 m); loosely rounded spread of branches roughly equal to half height

Range: From northern limit of tree growth across Canada and Alaska south to about U.S. border

Other common names: Canoe birch, white birch

The paper birch is a deciduous tree that grows quickly and is short-lived (few survive as long as 140 years). It is named for the white bark that peels from its trunk in horizontal strips. The twigs, bark, buds, and seeds are important food sources for a variety of wild animals. The tree's tough, waterproof bark has been used by native craftsmen to make canoes, baskets, and boxes. In the spring, the tree can be tapped to obtain sap from which syrup, beer, and medicinal tonics have been made. With its graceful form and striking white bark, the paper birch has become a popular landscaping tree.

ALASKA CEDAR / *Chamaecyparis nootkatensis*

Alaska cedar is one of the slowest-growing and longest-living conifers in northwestern North America. In regions rarely touched by forest fires or logging, it is not unusual to find individuals that are more than a thousand years old. The tree's narrow crown and flexible, drooping branches allow it to weather very heavy snow loads and even avalanches. The extremely durable and versatile wood is used for everything from specialty objects, such as toys and musical instruments, to industrial items as varied as boats and stadium seats. Most of the highest-quality logs are exported—many to Japan, where the wood of the Alaska cedar is very highly regarded.

Size: From 80 to 125 feet (24 to 38 m) in height

Range: With exception of few isolated stands, found within 100 miles (160 km) of Pacific Coast from northern California to Alaska

Other common names: Alaska yellow-cedar, Alaska cypress

WHITE CEDAR / *Thuja occidentalis*

Size: Reaches height of 40 to 50 feet (12 to 15 m), with diameter of 18 to 30 inches (45 to 75 cm)

Range: Southern Canada from Maritimes to Manitoba and northeastern U.S.

Other common names: Northern white cedar

The white cedar is a cold-climate conifer with a symmetrical pyramid shape. It is not a true cedar of the genus *Cedrus*, but in fact belongs to the genus *Thuja*. North American cedars were named for their pungent scent, which resembles the scent of the true cedars of Europe. A preparation made from the foliage of the white cedar was used by native North Americans to treat scurvy. When French explorers learned of the treatment, the tree became known as the tree of life. Today the wood is prized for its natural resistance to insects and decay, making it a good material for boats, shingles, and fence posts.

143

DOUGLAS-FIR / *Pseudotsuga menziesii*

One of the most important timber-producing conifers in the world, Douglas-fir often grows in pure stands, its dark green, short-needled foliage creating a dense canopy high above the forest floor. The sheer majesty of these towering trees has inspired conservation groups to campaign for their protection, while lumber interests point out that Douglas-fir regenerates quickly, making it a prolific, vital timber resource. Both points of view carry some weight. Although old-growth stands do indeed take centuries to mature, the species is by no means rare or endangered. In terms of standing biomass, coastal Douglas-fir and its Rocky Mountains variant represent the most plentiful single tree species in North America—possibly in the world.

Size: Coastal grows to height of 300 feet (90 m) or more, while diameter can exceed 10 feet (3 m); three times larger than Rocky Mountains subspecies *Pseudotsuga menziesii v. glauca*

Range: Coastal native from northern California to British Columbia; Rocky Mountains subspecies *P. menziesii v. glauca* extends from Alberta to north-central Mexico

BALSAM FIR / *Abies balsamea*

Size: Grows 40 to 60 feet (12 to 18 m) tall; diameter of 12 to 18 inches (30 to 45 cm)

Range: New England, New York, and southern Canada from Newfoundland to Alberta; subspecies *Abies phanerolepis* found as far south as Virginia

Other common names: Canada balsam, balsam, eastern fir

One of the most widespread conifers native to the mixed forests of eastern Canada, balsam fir is typically found in moist, low-lying areas. Its heavy lower branches offer many wildlife species shelter from wind and snow. Its needles are also an important food source for moose and deer, while its seeds are favored by small birds, squirrels, and chipmunks. A tight pyramid shape and fragrant needles make the balsam fir one of the most popular Christmas-tree species in eastern North America. Its needles are used to give the familiar balsam scent to soaps and other products.

EASTERN HEMLOCK / *Tsuga canadensis*

A tall, stately conifer, the eastern hemlock has a dense pyramidal crown. It is a slow-growing tree that may take three hundred years to reach maturity, then live five hundred or six hundred years. Unlike many trees, it grows well in the shade. Its needles are short and blunt and form two rows on opposite sides of the twig. The bark on mature trees is a dark purplish brown and deeply furrowed. At one time, huge numbers were harvested for their bark, which was used to make leather-tanning products. With the development of synthetic tanning products, the eastern hemlock is now used mostly to make pulp and newsprint.

Size: In typical stands, commonly grows to height of about 100 feet (30 m); tallest known specimen measured 160 feet (49 m) tall, with diameter of 7 feet (2 m)

Range: Eastern U.S., southeastern Canada

Other common names: Canada hemlock, hemlock spruce

RED MAPLE / *Acer rubrum*

Size: Grows 60 to 90 feet (18 to 27 m) high, with diameter of 18 to 30 inches (45 to 75 cm)

Range: Eastern U.S. and Canada

The red maple is one of the most widespread deciduous trees in eastern Canada and the United States in both boreal and temperate forests. It grows at a range of elevations and in many different soil conditions, doing best in the moist soil of ravines and gullies. The red maple is often found growing alongside the sugar maple. Both have the double-winged seeds typical of maples and a three- or five-lobed leaf (much like the five-lobed leaf featured on the Canadian flag). The tree is distinguished by its red buds, flowers, and leaf stems. Its brilliant red autumn foliage has made the tree a favorite planting along city streets and in suburban yards.

LODGEPOLE PINE / *Pinus contorta*

This widespread western conifer looks dramatically different depending on where it grows. On sand dunes and riverbanks and in bogs, the lodgepole pine is short and gnarled. In drier, inland areas it grows tall and straight. The lodgepole pine produces tough, woody cones that often remain unopened and attached to the tree for years. It is not unusual for the heat of a forest fire to open the cones, triggering a natural reforestation process. Following a forest fire, the trees grow in dense stands; otherwise, they tend to be farther apart. Lodgepole pines were used by native North Americans to build teepees.

Size: Coastal 20 to 40 feet (6 to 12 m) tall, inland up to 100 feet (30 m) tall; diameter ranges from 6 to 20 inches (15 to 50 cm)

Range: From Yukon to Baja peninsula near coast and in Rocky Mountains east as far as South Dakota

RED PINE / *Pinus resinosa*

Size: Average height ranges from 65 to 100 feet (20 to 30 m); diameter of trunk reaches 35 inches (90 cm)

Range: Zone about 1,500 miles (2,400 km) long and 500 miles (800 km) wide along Great Lakes and St. Lawrence River

Other common names: Norway pine

A tall conifer with dark foliage, the red pine has a smooth, straight trunk and reddish-colored bark. Its needles grow in bundles of two. They measure four to six inches (9 to 12 cm) long and snap easily when bent. The cones are one to two inches (2 to 5 cm) long. Each year the tree adds another whorl, or layer of branches, to its lengthening trunk. It commonly grows on dry, sandy soils. The resinous and relatively strong wood of red pine is used in construction and for railway ties and pulp production. The tree is one of the most extensively planted species in the northern United States and Canada.

WESTERN WHITE PINE / *Pinus monticola*

A tall conifer with a small crown and slender, bluish-green needles, the western white pine is an important timber tree. Its soft, straight-grained wood is ideal for a range of millwork applications, including doors, shelving, window sashes, and shutters. The white pine is important for a variety of wildlife species as well. It provides shelter for small animals and its seeds are a key food for rodents and small birds. The tree is also a favorite of bears, which claw the bark to get at the sweet sap, sometimes damaging the tree so badly it cannot survive.

Size: Generally 100 to 160 feet (30 to 50 m), but can exceed 200 feet (60 m); diameter ranges from 3 to 7 feet (1 to 2 m)

Range: Western U.S. and Canada; most common in northern Rockies

Other common names: White pine, Idaho white pine

BALSAM POPLAR / *Populus balsamifera*

Size: Reaches average height of 80 to 100 feet (25 to 30 m)

Range: Broad band above Canada–U.S. border stretching from eastern Canada to northwest Alaska

Other common names: Cottonwood, Balm-of-Gilead, tacamahac

The hardy balsam poplar thrives along stream banks in northern regions, including areas too harsh for most other trees. It is fast-growing and relatively short-lived, only occasionally surviving as long as two hundred years. The topside of the tree's leaves is green, the underside is silvery white. During spring, the large, sticky buds of the balsam poplar produce a pungent fragrance. Extracts from winter buds were recognized by native peoples as having therapeutic value. For example, a salve to relieve congestion was made by heating the buds in oil. Today the poplar is used for pulp and veneer. Many animals, such as deer and moose, eat the tree's twigs.

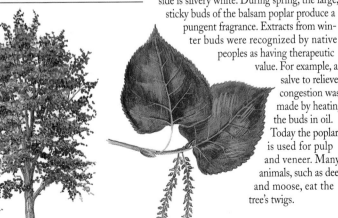

BLACK SPRUCE / *Picea mariana*

The black spruce is a wide-ranging and abundant conifer. It usually grows in wet, organic soils, such as on the muskegs of northern Canada, where black spruce is the dominant tree species. Red squirrels feast on the tips of lower cone-bearing branches. Black spruce is Canada's most important pulpwood species: The long fibers in the wood make for particularly strong paper. Native groups have had many traditional uses for the black spruce, including making a medicinal salve from the tree's resin, beverages from the twigs and needles, and binding material for birch-bark canoes from the roots.

Size: On favorable sites, height ranges from 40 to 65 feet (12 to 20 m); on poor sites, from 25 to 40 feet (7.5 to 12 m)

Range: Canada, Alaska and northern U.S.

Other common names: Bog spruce, swamp spruce

SITKA SPRUCE / *Picea sitchensis*

Size: Grows 130 to 200 feet (40 to 60 m) high, sometimes taller; diameter ranges from 3 to 10 feet (1 to 3 m)

Range: Fifty-mile (80-km) -wide band along U.S. and Canada west coast from Alaska to northern California

This massive conifer is the largest spruce in the world. The tree thrives at river mouths and in swampy areas, though its range extends to rocky shorelines, where it clings to crags with huge, buttressed roots. Sitka spruce can live up to eight hundred years and reach a height of well over two hundred feet (60 m). Lightweight and exceptionally strong, the wood is suitable for a range of applications, from general construction to making soundboards in musical instruments. During World Wars I and II, it was a standard material in aircraft manufacturing. The Sitka spruce is one of the most commonly planted trees in northern Europe.

WHITE SPRUCE / *Picea glauca*

The white spruce is a familiar sight in the forests of Alaska and northern Canada. It grows slowly and may live as long as a thousand years in the northern part of its range. The needles and young shoots emit a disagreeable odor when bruised—hence the common names cat and skunk spruce—but are a valuable food source in winter for a variety of wildlife. White spruce grows in a wide range of temperature and soil conditions, from the Arctic Circle, where the soil is never free from frost, to the northern United States, where summer temperatures may exceed ninety-five degrees Fahrenheit (35°C).

Size: Reaches height of roughly 100 feet (30 m) In warmer regions; stunted closer to tree line

Range: Throughout Canada (except for Pacific Coast) and in northeastern U.S.

Other common names: Canadian spruce, cat spruce, skunk spruce

TAMARACK / *Larix laricina*

Size: Typically grows to height of 50 to 80 feet (15 to 25 m); occasionally tops 115 feet (35 m)

Range: Northern Canada south to northeastern U.S. and west-central Canada

Other common names: Larch, hackmatack

Although the tamarack is a conifer and looks like an evergreen, it sheds its needles every autumn. The soft, flat needles grow in dense clusters; they are bright green in the spring, blue-green in summer, and yellow in the autumn. The tree grows most commonly in wet, organic soil, such as peat bogs. In swamps, tamaracks develop strong and very long fibrous roots that native craftsmen traditionally used to sew pieces of birch bark together to make canoes. The wood is very resinous and resistant to rotting, making for good fence posts. Tamarack forests are sometimes severely damaged by larvae of the larch sawfly, which feed on the foliage.

Rain Forest

The defining criteria for a rain forest are not clearly established, but the key underlying principle is that it is based on virtually ideal year-round growing conditions, with constantly high relative humidity and exceptionally regular precipitation, often in the form of daily cloudbursts. Frost never occurs and the temperature remains continually warm throughout the year. In fact, in some rain forests, seasonal cycles in the mean daily temperature do not vary above or below the average range of daily highs and lows. So conducive are these conditions to the growth of plant life that they could hardly be bettered in even the most carefully controlled greenhouse.

The more extensive rain forests of the world tend to be distributed along the equator, through the Amazon basin of South America and across central Africa, Southeast Asia, and Indonesia. Their reach further north or south of the equator is made possible by the moderating effects of maritime climates such as those found in Central America and along the northeast coast of Australia. Rain forests are generally associated with low elevations, where humidity and temperature remain most constant, but there are numerous exceptions. For example, the highlands of Central America are home to cloud forests made possible by condensation as moist ocean winds are uplifted.

DIVERSITY AND INTERDEPENDENCE

One of the most unusual examples of what is often deemed a rain forest is found on the Olympic Peninsula in Washington state. The prevailing winds coming off the North Pacific keep it humid and perpetually saturated, while its maritime location moderates the extreme seasonal variation in temperatures typical of this northerly latitude. And yet despite these almost ideal growing conditions, the forest lacks what all tropical rain forests possess: a tremendous diversity of its composition in terms of number of species and also their interdependence. While several acres of a well-endowed temperate forest may contain a dozen or so species of trees, a similarly small area of tropical rain forest could easily contain upward of ten times as many species.

The equatorial rain forests are arguably the oldest continuously forested regions on Earth. Having been spared the scouring effects of recent Ice Ages, these forests have been evolving for tens, if not hundreds, of millions of years, with no devastating change in climate to deter them. As a result, they host the greatest diversity of botanical families and a disproportionate share of the more recently evolved species.

Internally, rain forests are on the one hand intensely competitive environments and yet among the most fragile of all biomes. With moisture in abundance, the primary competition centers on the struggle for available sunlight and nutrients. Each species of tree has adapted to compete for sunlight by becoming a constituent of one of the forest's multiple canopy layers. Each layer relies on a host of adaptive characteristics to take advantage of its place in the forest, from xylem tissue strength to shade tolerance. Even seeding characteristics are affected. Take the Brazilnut tree (*Bertholletia excelsa*), for example. This top-canopy species has fruit with a dozen or so nuts contained inside a softball-sized sphere weighing a pound (0.5 kg) or more. The heavy weight of the fruit allows it to plummet down through the lower canopies, where it literally explodes on the forest floor from the impact, scattering the nuts.

The tropical rain forests are nature's experimental laboratories, expanding the plant kingdom's diversity and radiating out new species, which often eventually expand their range to enrich adjacent biomes.

The use of available sunlight by the various layers of arboreal species is remarkably efficient. In fact, the floor of a typical rain forest is an exceptionally uncluttered place. Even the accumulation of fallen leaves and other litter commonly found on the floor of temperate forests is not seen in rain forests because of the extremely rapid decomposition and recycling of all available nutrients.

A VULNERABLE WORLD

The great diversity of species within a rain forest, the finely tuned balance with which this community of living things operates, and the efficiency it achieves in utilizing its available resources define it as one of nature's most marvelous accomplishments. However, these very attributes make it fragile and exceptionally vulnerable to outside interference. The selective removal of any given species endangers other species, which depend on its former contribution to the community for their survival, even if that contribution was merely the shade it provided.

Also, rain forests that are totally cut or burned do not regenerate easily, at least not to the full extent of their previous diversity. The abundant rainfall, which made their existence possible in the first place, quickly leaches and erodes the unprotected soil. Once a rain forest is gone, it is gone for at least centuries, if not millennia.

INDIAN ALMOND / *Terminalia catappa*

A tall deciduous or partially deciduous tree that favors wet, monsoonal regions, the Indian almond is unrelated to the more familiar almond of the genus *Prunus*. *Terminalia catappa* was named for its delicately flavored seeds, which resemble the true almond. The seeds are preceded by spikes of greenish-white flowers that give off an unpleasant odor. The Indian almond displays a unique branching pattern in which branches radiate from the trunk in layers—each one the same length and at the same distance from its neighbors. Trees that grow in this way are sometimes referred to as "pagoda trees" and the branching pattern has been given the Indian almond's genus name *Terminalia*.

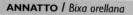

Size: Grows to 40 to 60 feet (12 to 18 m), with diameter of 24 to 36 inches (60 to 90 cm)

Range: Native to Malaya, but naturalized in many parts of tropics

ANNATTO / *Bixa orellana*

Size: Shrub or small tree from 7 to 20 feet (2 to 6 m) tall

Range: Native to Central and South America; also cultivated in other tropical regions of Asia and India

Other common names: Achiote, urucum, lipstick tree

The annatto is a common tropical tree with seed capsules that produce a widely used red pigment. The tree is well-adapted to poor or acidic soils. It has triangular leaves, large pink flowers, and produces clusters of scarlet, heart-shaped pods. When mature, the pods split open to reveal seeds covered with a sticky, orange-red pulp or resin called "bixin." Seeds are stirred in water to prepare the dye that is used to color butter, cheese, and the tamales in Latin American cooking. This pigment has been used by natives of the Amazon for centuries as protection from the sun and to treat insect stings.

BALSA / *Ochroma pyramidale*

This fast-growing evergreen produces the world's lightest commercial lumber. Best known for its use in crafts such as model-airplane building, balsa wood lends itself to a wide range of other applications where light weight or buoyancy is required. These include floats for fishing nets, surfboards, theatrical props, and soundproofing. The balsa tree has a slender trunk and an open crown. Its large leaves are heart-shaped with reddish stalks and the flowers are white or greenish and bell-shaped. The white or pinkish wood can be harvested when the tree is only five years old. Unlike most commercial timbers, balsa is most prized for its sapwood, not its heartwood. As a result, early harvest of fast-grown trees produces superior, lightweight balsa wood.

Size: Grows to 80 to 90 feet (24 to 27 m) tall, with diameter of 12 to 14 inches (30 to 35 cm), occasionally up to 36 inches (90 cm)

Range: Central and South America as far south as southern Brazil

BRAZILNUT / *Bertholletia excelsa*

Size: Up to 165 feet (50 m) in height, with diameter of 3 to 7 feet (1 to 2 m)

Range: Northern South America; planted in other rain-forest regions

Other common names: Para nut

A large evergreen tree, the Brazilnut is well-known for its delicious, white-fleshed kernels. The trees develop long, straight trunks and have bright-green, leathery leaves that are often fourteen inches (35 cm) long. Large, round, woody pods take twelve to fourteen months to mature and grow to about the size of a melon. The pods are cut at one end to extract the twelve to twenty-four triangular nuts packed inside. The individual Brazilnuts have to be cracked to obtain the large kernel, which is the edible part. With 66 percent fat—one of the highest levels of all nuts—and 14 percent protein, the kernels are a rich and highly nutritious food.

153

CACAO / *Theobroma cacao*

Relished around the world, chocolate is produced from the seeds of a small evergreen of the Americas. The seeds grow in foot-long, ribbed red pods. Ancient peoples of Central and South America used the seeds as currency. They also roasted and ground them and mixed them with spices to make a thick beverage referred to as "chocolatl." With European colonization of the Americas, the cacao tree began to be cultivated around the world. Linnaeus gave the genus the appropriate name *Theobroma*, or "food of the gods." Both cocoa and chocolate are produced from the roasted and ground seeds, but cocoa has much of the fat, or "cocoa butter," removed, while chocolate is made by retaining the fat.

Size: Up to 40 feet (12 m) tall

Range: Tropical Central and South America

CASSIA / *Cassia fistula*

Size: Ranges in height from 20 to 30 feet (6 to 9 m)

Range: Native to India, but grown throughout tropics

Other common names: Indian laburnum, pudding-pipe tree

This handsome tree of monsoonal forests is grown primarily for its brilliant yellow flowers and graceful foliage. It has a straight trunk and spreading branches with compound leaves that are eight to sixteen inches (20 to 40 cm) long. The flowers appear when branches are bare and hang down in delicate clusters like a shower of golden petals. The fruit is a very large pod that may be up to three feet (1 m) long and twelve inches (30 cm) thick. In some countries, the pods and twigs are used for fodder, while the hard and very heavy wood is well-suited for cabinetmaking.

COLATREE / Cola acuminata

This species is one of a group of tropical African trees that produces cola nuts. *Cola acuminata* is a narrow tree with branches that originate at the base and an open, spreading crown. The leaves are elliptical and the flowers are white or yellow-ish, dotted with purple. The fruits have podlike sections containing numerous seeds or nuts that are a source of caffeine and other stimulants. They are chewed by African peoples to promote digestion and to relieve fatigue. They are also used as an ingredient in medications and beverages. The colatree is of the same family as the cacao tree of the Americas.

Size: Reaches height of about 40 feet (12 m)

Range: West and central tropical Africa

CORDIA / Cordia subcordata

Size: A small- to medium-sized tree that grows 27 feet (8 m) tall on average

Range: Parts of Southeast Asia, India, East Africa, Madagascar, Polynesia

The cordia tree is a quick-growing evergreen with a thick, wide crown of leaves that make it a favorite shade tree. The leaves are a glossy green, oval in shape, and about four inches (10 cm) long. Its attractive, bell-shaped orange flowers are scentless and popular in Hawaii for making leis. The round, green fruits change to yellow and black as they dry and contain a stone with one to four seeds. The wood is prized for its beautiful grain, which is light golden with dark, often purple markings that make it attractive for carving. It was also used by the early Polynesians to make utensils, bowls, and canoes.

155

BIGLEAF MAHOGANY / *Swietenia macrophylla*

Mahogany is world-renowned for its beautifully grained, durable wood, making it the most valuable timber species in tropical Central and South America. The small, yellow-white flowers are borne in loose clusters at the end of the dry season. Fruits are woody capsules that contain up to forty wind-dispersed seeds. Mahogany was first used around 1500 for building ships, but soon became very popular for making furniture, paneling, and pianos. The wood is decay-resistant and swells and shrinks little with changes in humidity. Although mahogany is widely distributed, it regenerates slowly and there is concern that present logging practices may wipe out large stands of the tree.

Size: A very tall tree, up to 165 feet (50 m) in height, with trunk diameter of 7 feet (2 m) or larger

Range: Mexico, Central America, and northern South America

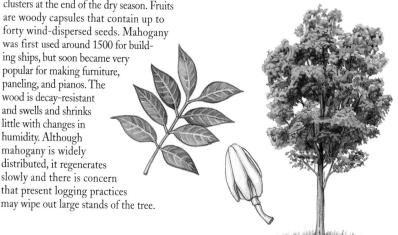

ORCHID TREE / *Bauhinia variegata*

Size: A small tree from 17 to 23 feet (5 to 7 m) tall

Range: Native to tropical Asia, but grows well in all tropical countries

Other common names: Mountain ebony

As its name suggests, the orchid tree produces a spectacular, dense covering of orchid-shaped blossoms. The faintly fragrant flowers may be five inches (12 cm) in diameter and have four narrow petals of pale pink and a fifth top petal streaked with red or purple. There are also varieties with white blossoms and yellow streaks. The deep-green leaves are also distinctive. Each rounded leaf is so deeply cleft that it seems like twin leaves joined in the middle. This structure accounts for the tree's Latin name, which honors Jean and Gaspard Bauhin, twin Swiss botanists who worked together so closely that the twin leaflets were thought to symbolize their work.

AFRICAN PADAUK / *Pterocarpus soyauxii*

This genus is named *Pterocarpus* because of the winged seeds typical of its members. The various *Pterocarpus* species are the source of some of the world's most beautiful, vivid red woods, used for cabinetmaking, turning, flooring, decorative veneer, and tool and knife handles. African padauk is a durable wood that is more readily available than Andaman padauk (*P. dalbergioides*), one of the world's rarest hardwoods. When cut or shaped by power tools, African padauk—like many exotic woods—gives off a fine sawdust that can cause respiratory problems.

Size: Ranges from 100 to 130 feet (30 to 40 m) tall, with diameter of up to 5 feet (1.5 m)

Range: Central and West Africa

Other common names: Barwood, camwood, ngula, bosulu

PURPLEHEART / *Peltogyne paniculata*

Size: A tall, buttressed tree up to 130 feet (40 m) in height

Range: Mexico, Central and South America

Other common names: Amaranth, violetwood

Purpleheart is a tall, handsome tree that produces one of the most distinctive woods in the world. When freshly cut, the heartwood is a light, dull brown, but within minutes the surface changes to an astonishing bright purple. With further exposure to sunlight, it gradually takes on a dark, chocolate-purple color. Purpleheart is used for furniture, veneers, and butts of billiard cues. The tree has pinnate leaves, small leaflets that are in pairs on each side of a stem, and small white or pink flowers in drooping clusters, or panicles. Purpleheart has been exploited extensively for years and is increasingly rare in parts of its original range.

RUBBERTREE / *Hevea brasiliensis*

The rubbertree (not to be confused with the rubber plant, *Ficus elastica*, commonly grown as a house plant) is the primary source of natural rubber. A native of the Amazon basin, *Hevea brasiliensis* is a tall deciduous tree, with leaves on long stalks and fragrant, yellowish flowers. Rubber is produced by making cuts in the bark, releasing the liquid latex. The latex is then used in liquid form or coagulated with acid to make rubber. Until the end of the nineteenth century, rubber was produced exclusively from trees in their natural setting. Today rubbertrees are cultivated extensively on plantations in other parts of the tropics, particularly Indonesia and Malaysia.

Size: Up to 100 feet (30 m) tall

Range: South America, primarily the Amazon basin, and in tropical plantations worldwide

SALTREE / *Shorea robusta*

Size: Reaches height of 100 feet (30 m) or more

Range: Southeast Asia, India, and parts of Bangladesh and Myanmar

This Southeast Asia tree, like about a third of the species belonging to the genus *Shorea*, is a source of the wood known as lauan. A popular hardwood, lauan ranges in color from light brown to dark red. Depending on the species and growing conditions, the wood may range in density from as soft as basswood to as dense as white oak. It is commonly compared to mahogany and often even referred to as "Philippine mahogany." Lauan is popular as paneling, cabinetry, furniture, and interior trim, and is also commonly used in the manufacture of plywood. The trees of the genus typically have broadly buttressed trunks that may be branchless up to a height of sixty feet (18 m). Various species of *Shorea* are found in both rain and monsoonal forests.

SANDBOX TREE / *Hura crepitans*

A relative of the rubbertree, the tall sandbox tree is characterized by a dense arrangement of large, fleshy, oddly shaped flowers. The tree protects ripening seed pods with sap so toxic that it causes red welts when it comes in contact with human skin and blindness if rubbed in the eye. Still, the pods have one animal predator: the macaw. After it fearlessly tears into unripe seed pods, this brightly colored bird detoxifies itself by eating calcium-rich clay from nearby riverbanks. The clay is thought to absorb the poisonous alkaloids present in the fruit.

Size: Typically reaches height of 90 to 130 feet (27 to 40 m), with diameter of 3 to 7 feet (1 to 2 m)

Range: Throughout West Indies and from Central America to northern Brazil

Other common names: Possumwood

ZEBRAWOOD / *Microberlinia brazzavillensis*

Size: Grows to height of 165 feet (50 m), with trunk diameter above buttresses of 5 feet (1.5 m)

Range: West Africa, especially Gabon, Cameroon, and the Congo

Other common names: Zebrano, zingana

Zebrawood is named for its highly unusual wood, which features contrasting bands of light yellow-gold and dark brown to black, like the stripes of a zebra. The wood can be hard, strong, and dense, while the grain is interlocked and wavy, making it difficult to work with. The wood polishes to a high luster and is prized for making small decorative pieces, veneers, and guitars. Zebrawood comes from a small area of West Africa, where it is found along riverbanks and other places where its roots have an abundant supply of water. Harvesting is often difficult because of its great height and large buttresses and because it often grows in inaccessible areas.

Tidal Zones, Shores, & Swamps

Most terrestrial biomes present some limitation in the availability of moisture. Even when total annual precipitation is abundant, it is often seasonally restricted and the plant species in these biomes have developed ways to deal with periods of scarcity. But, the perpetually saturated soil of tidal zones, shores, and swamps provides even greater challenges to plant and tree life. Only tree species with highly adapted root systems thrive in these places, which include inland freshwater swamps, brackish (semi-salty) swamps, tidal zones next to river estuaries, and ocean shores saturated with saltwater. The native trees include some of the most primitive conifers, such as baldcypress (*Taxodium distichum*), as well as the more advanced angiosperms, including many palms (*Palmae*), tupelo (*Nyssa*), and mangrove (*Rhizophora*).

With the exception of a few relatively extensive swamp regions, the biome tends to be transitional, forming thin bands along low-lying shores or in the flood plains of rivers. It also tends to be a closely knit community, not subject to the incursion of terrestrial species from adjacent biomes. Either a species thrives with its roots in perpetually wet soil or it lives elsewhere.

In addition to unusual root systems, other more subtle but equally important adaptations allow these trees to colonize swampy soils. With the high water table in these environments, there is no need for deeply penetrating taproots. But shallow root systems provide poor anchorage in the mucky soil. To make up for this, many species in this biome develop a swollen lower bowl, or buttress. The wide girth of the buttress helps guard against toppling—and may provide other functions as well, although this is not well established. The mangroves of the tidal zones are adapted in another way. Confronted by the rush of advancing and receding tides, they have evolved extensive stiltlike root systems.

Trees living in swamps have evolved various strategies for coping with something that would spell death to most arboreal species—continual emersion in water.

BALDCYPRESS / *Taxodium distichum*

The baldcypress thrives in swampy areas, its branches often draped with Spanish moss. The tree's light-green needles turn yellow or orange in the autumn and fall from the tree. The trunk is flared at the base. When it grows in water, the baldcypress develops "knees," cone-shaped appendages that rise from the roots. Knees protrude from the ground anywhere from an inch to several feet—depending on the average water level of the site—and help provide air to the roots of the tree. The baldcypress is an important timber species and the heartwood from a mature tree resists decay very well.

Size: From 100 to 165 feet (30 to 50 m) high with flat-topped crown at maturity

Range: Southeastern U.S. in swamps, in coastal areas, and along riverbanks

Other common names: Swamp cypress

BEEFWOOD / *Casuarina equisetifolia*

Size: Up to 150 feet (45 m) tall, with diameter of 24 to 36 inches (60 to 90 cm); because it is often grown in open as seashore cultivar, height of 80 to 100 feet (24.5 to 30 m) more common

Range: Native to Australia, Southeast Asia, and East Indies, but widely planted elsewhere in tropical and subtropical regions

Other common names: South Seas ironwood, Australian pine, she-oak

In Australia, this species goes by the name of she-oak because the prominent ray flecks in its wood are similar to those in the true oaks (*Quercus* spp.). Casuarina is not at all closely related to the oaks and is, in fact, a rather curious oddity in the plant kingdom. Its conelike woody fruit and long strands of scaly "leaves" make it look like a conifer, but most botanists classify it as an angiosperm. Even among the angiosperms, it is unique in having numerous embryo sacs in each ovule, placing it in its own separate order, the Casuarinales. Although frost-sensitive, *Casuarina* is otherwise very hardy, tolerating saturated soil and high concentrations of salt.

COCONUT PALM / *Cocos nucifera*

The coconut palm is the most familiar of the palms and a symbol of the tropics. Its tall trunk is marked with distinctive, semicircular scars from the fallen leaves and is topped with feathery fronds as long as sixteen feet (5 m). The fruit grows to about a foot (0.3 m) across and contains the seed that we know as the coconut. *Cocos nucifera* is one of the most useful trees to humans. The fiber from the fruit can be turned into matting. The flesh of the seed is eaten and is a source of oil, while the fronds are used for thatch and basketry.

Size: Grows 50 to 80 feet (15 to 24 m) tall, with diameter of 12 to 20 inches (30 to 50 cm)

Range: Likely native to Southeast Asia, but now grows along coastlines in many tropical regions

FISH-POISON-TREE / *Piscidia piscipula*

Size: Up to 50 feet (15 m) tall, with diameter of 3 feet (1 m)

Range: Southern tip of Florida and Mexico

Other common names: Jamaica dogwood

The unusual name of this tree comes from a substance found in the bark of the roots and in young branches and leaves, which is used by people of the Caribbean to poison or stupefy fish so they can be easily picked up from the surface of the water. The fish-poison-tree has compound leaves that are hairy below and shiny and dark-green above. The clustered flowers appear in spring and are white, tinged with red. The fruit is a pod, up to four inches (10 cm) long, with four thin, wavy wings along the edge. The wood is hard-grained and moisture-resistant and is used for shipbuilding, posts, and wood carving.

RED MANGROVE / *Rhizophora mangle*

An evergreen tree that grows in brackish water or saltwater, the red mangrove is characterized by "stilt roots" that grow from the trunk and lower branches. These roots project above the water at least some of the time to allow for the exchanges of gases necessary for the tree's survival. The tangle of roots also catches soil and debris and protects the shoreline from storms, as well as providing a crucial habitat for fish and shellfish. The fruit is a cone-shaped brown berry with a short tube, through which a developing green root grows. When the seedlings drop, they may float long distances in ocean currents before taking root on distant shores.

Size: Rarely more than 25 feet (7.5 m) tall in Florida, but up to 80 feet (24.5 m) tall in tropical regions, often forming impenetrable thickets

Range: Throughout neotropics and also along west coast of tropical Africa

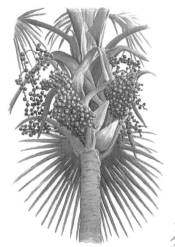

LATAN PALM / *Latania loddigesii*

Size: Reaches height of 30 feet (9 m)

Range: Native to Mauritius

Other common names: Blue Latin palm

This striking palm is topped with up to a dozen large, fan-shaped fronds, each with about thirty segments. The tree is sometimes referred to as a "blue Latin palm" because of the distinctive bluish color of the stems and veins of the younger leaves. Latan palms tend to grow on cliffs or in canyons near the shore where they can benefit from the humidity without being directly exposed to salt spray.

SCREW PINE / *Pandanus tectorius*

The screw pine, a common palmlike tree found along the rocky shores of Polynesian islands and atolls, ranks second only to the coconut palm in local economic importance. Conspicuous prop roots at the base of the trunk support these trees in water-logged soils and in strong winds. The long, narrow leaves have saw-toothed edges and a row of spines running down the central leaf spine. When the spines are removed, the fibrous, flexible leaf provides a strong material well-suited for making baskets, mats, and thatching for houses. Large, multiple fruits, resembling pineapples, may be bright orange or red and are often polished for use in necklaces or leis.

Size: Grows as bush or small, many-branched tree from 23 to 30 feet (7 to 9 m) tall, often in thickets

Range: Polynesia, India, tropical Asia

Other common names: Hala, pandan

RAMIN / *Gonystylus bancanus*

Size: Reaches height of 140 feet (42 m)

Range: Grows at low to medium elevations in peat swamp forests in Malaysia and certain Indonesian islands, such as Sumatra

This small to medium-size tree generally has no branches on the lower half of its trunk. It produces flowers and fruits at frequent but irregular intervals. Ramin is one of the major export timbers of Southeast Asia. The wood is a relatively lightweight and versatile hardwood. Some woodworkers rely on it as a substitute for beech to make furniture, fittings, and moldings. It is also used for carving, wooden toys, turnings, dowels, and flooring.

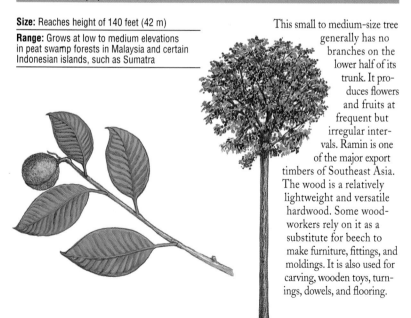

SEA GRAPE / *Cocoloba uvifera*

This small evergreen is well adapted to life along the sea coast. It thrives in sandy soils and is resistant to wind and salt spray. Growing on sand dunes, it plays an important role in preventing erosion. The sea grape has large, leathery leaves with prominent red veins and produces small, fragrant, white flowers. It owes its common name to the clusters of purple or greenish fruits that it produces. The fruits have a sweetish, acidic taste and can be eaten or made into wine or jellies. The sea grape is often planted as an ornamental in coastal areas.

Size: Grows to maximum height of 35 feet (11 m)

Range: Native to coastal regions of tropical America

WATER TUPELO / *Nyssa aquatica*

Size: Up to 75 feet (23 m) tall at good sites, with 24-inch (60-cm) -diameter trunk above buttress

Range: Southeastern U.S. in swamps and river basins

Other common names: Swamp tupelo, cottongum, sourgum

The water tupelo is a large, long-lived tree that grows best in swampy areas. The large, pale leaves have very few angular teeth and turn a brilliant maroon-brown in the autumn before they fall. The solitary, greenish-white flowers are inconspicuous, but are a source of tupelo honey. Fruits are oblong and dark purple with pale dots when mature and contain a bony, ribbed stone. Since the water tupelo is one of the few tree species that can survive extended periods of flooding, it is favored for planting in very wet sites.

Savanna & Chaparral

Savanna and chapparal are biomes where trees exist and yet are not found in forests. Two of the more common species found in this biome in Africa are the acacia (left) and the baobab (right).

In a biome dominated by shrubs and grasses, any tree has a clear advantage in the struggle to capture sunlight. But this advantage depends on a tree's ability to maintain a continuous column of sap in its vascular tissue—the lifeline of perennial, arboreal growth. This can prove difficult in areas such as savannas and chaparral, with their brief wet season and almost constant state of drought. Such a life zone favors shrubs and grasses, which die back to ground level when water is scarce or germinate at the onset of the wet season. In this biome, trees struggle to maintain a presence and it is a tribute to their adaptability that they succeed even in a marginal way.

Savanna and chaparral are found in both the tropical and temperate zones and include the sub-Saharan savanna of Africa, the oak grove savannas of east-central North America and California's Coast Ranges and Sierra Nevada foothills,

Australia's Outback, and the chaparral regions of the southwestern United States, Mexico, and southern South America.

While savanna and chapparal regions share similarities in terms of scant and seasonal precipitation, the tree species they host vary greatly, especially in terms of adaptive strategies. For example, the acacia and baobab trees of Africa's savanna tend to be widely spaced in a parklike setting, counting on their extensive and efficient root systems to capture moisture, while the tap-rooted oaks of America's oak-grove prairies congregate where the water table is high or where the bedrock creates natural cisterns.

Many chaparral regions are, in effect, would-be forests populated by some species capable of much greater stature, but kept in a perpetual state of impenetrable, shrubby thickets, scorched and forced to recycle by occasional dry-season brushfires.

BAOBAB / *Adansonia digitata*

This immense deciduous tree is, for many, the symbol of Africa. It has a barrel-like trunk and its short, thick branches resemble roots, inspiring the legend that the gods planted the mighty tree upside down. The baobab has a multitude of uses for both humans and animals. Animals make their home in the trunk and branches, while elephants dig the moist pulp from the tree's base. Trunks that have been hollowed out by elephants are used by people for water storage and sometimes for shelter. Both the palmlike leaves and sausage-shaped fruits are edible. The fibrous bark is used for ropes and basketry, and the tree has the unusual ability to replace the bark as it is stripped away.

Size: Grows to 75 feet (22 m) in height, with diameter of up to 30 feet (9 m)

Range: Throughout African savannas

Other common names: Monkey bread tree

FREMONT COTTONWOOD / *Populus fremontii*

A tall, fast-growing deciduous tree, the Fremont cottonwood owes its common name to the tufts of white fluff that aid in dispersing its seeds. Male and female catkins are produced on separate trees and seed production is so abundant that a single female tree can carpet five hundred square feet (46 sq m) with "cotton," causing the tree to be outlawed in some communities. Fremont cottonwoods grow in moist areas near waterways and are often an indication of underground water. Dispersal of the seeds on streams and rivers is so important to the survival of the trees that they are often threatened by human interference in water courses.

Size: Grows to 100 feet (30 m) in height, with diameter of more than 3 feet (1 m)

Range: Along California coast and in lowlands of Southwest

MESQUITE / *Prosopis juliflora*

Size: In most arid regions usually shrub, but with adequate water can reach 50 feet (15 m) in height with diameter of 3 feet (1 m)

Range: Native to southwest U.S., Mexico, Central America, and Caribbean, but planted worldwide in hot, dry regions

The mesquite is a common and useful tree of hot, arid regions. It has spiny branches, pinnate leaves composed of many very small leaflets, and greenish-white, fragrant flowers. The narrow seed pods are sweet and an important source of forage. Mesquite shrubs may develop enormous underground stems called "cepas," which serve as firewood in areas where little else is available. At one time, wood from the mesquite was used for railway cross-ties and fence posts and the bark and wood provided an ingredient for tanning. The inner bark of the root supplied fiber for coarse fabric, while an amber-colored gum exuded from the trunk was used in medicines.

BUR OAK / *Quercus macrocarpa*

One of the largest oaks of North America, the bur oak has a massive trunk and a broad crown. Its leaves can be distinguished from those of other oaks by the deep lobes near the center that appear to cut the leaf in two. Although the bur oak will tolerate a variety of soil types and moisture conditions, it is known as the oak of the prairies. Its extensive root system makes it one of the most drought-resistant of the oaks, while its thick, corky bark enables it to survive prairie fires. Open groves of bur oaks were favorite sites for early homesteaders.

Size: Grows to height of 65 to 130 feet (20 to 40 m), with diameter of up to 7 feet (2 m)

Range: Throughout American Midwest and north into southern Canada

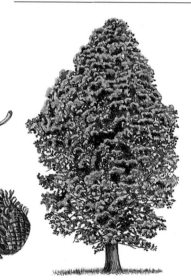

PEPPERTREE / *Schinus molle*

Size: Grows to 50 feet (15 m) in height

Range: Native to Peru

Other common names: California pepper tree, Peruvian mastic tree

This graceful evergreen has a rounded crown and somewhat pendulous branches. The feathery leaves are made up of numerous small leaflets. The tiny, yellowish flowers grow in clusters, with male and female flowers on separate trees, and the berrylike fruit that follows is rosy red. The fragrant seeds are used in Mexico to flavor beverages and occasionally elsewhere as an additive in black pepper. The peppertree is popular as a shade tree and often becomes naturalized in areas with dry, sandy soil. Its resinous bark gives the tree its alternate name of Peruvian mastic tree.

PINYON / *Pinus edulis*

Size: From 15 to 50 feet (4.5 to 15 m) tall, with broad crown almost as wide as tree's height

Range: Predominates in pinyon-juniper woodlands of semi-desert zone of southwestern U.S.

Other common names: Colorado pinyon, nut pine

A long-lived tree of dry, rocky soils, the pinyon derives its name from the Spanish word for pine nuts, *piñones*. The tree's nuts are large and have a delicate flavor enjoyed by both birds and people. Nuts are commonly consumed after roasting in the shell, but can be eaten raw. Several species of jays feast on the seeds and do much of the seed dispersal. Pinyon jays can carry fifty seeds at a time in their throat and tend to cache large amounts for consumption during the winter months. Some of these buried seeds are not recovered by the birds and provide an important source for germination.

TAMARIND / *Tamarindus indica*

The tamarind tree is cultivated extensively throughout much of India as a shade tree as well as for its fruit. It is a tall tree with massive trunk and branches. The flowers are yellow with pink stripes and the fruit takes the form of brown pods, the acidic pulp of which is used as a flavoring in foods and beverages. The tamarind can be either deciduous or evergreen. In dry areas, it sometimes loses its leaves briefly during the hottest part of the year. Its feathery leaves close up after sunset and in chilly, damp weather.

Size: Grows to 80 feet (24 m) in height, with diameter of up to 7 feet (1 m)

Range: Origin uncertain, but cultivated or naturalized throughout Indian subcontinent

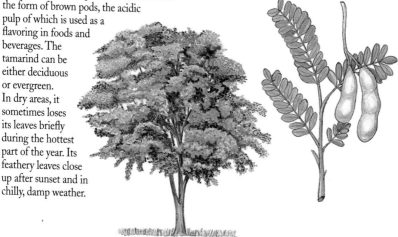

BLACK WATTLE / *Acacia mearnsii*

Size: From 20 to 65 feet (6 to 20 m) in height; can sprout from base of trunk and form impenetrable thickets

Range: Native to southeast Australia and Tasmania, but planted widely throughout world

The black wattle is cultivated for its tannin-rich bark. The tree grows rapidly and provides bark five to ten years after seeding. The bark is stripped from the tree and cut into three-foot (1-m) lengths, dried and baled, and sold to the leather industry. The black wattle has many small, green leaflets, tiny, pale flowers, and gray-brown pods. It thrives in poor dry soils and its roots, which take nitrogen from the air and convert it into a mineral in the ground—a process called nitrogen fixing—can help to improve soil quality.

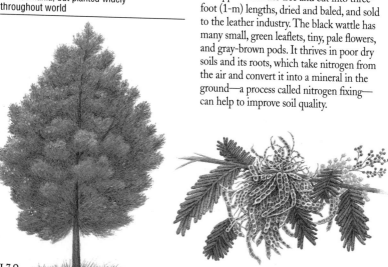

Desert

In some of the world's driest deserts, the typical interval between any precipitation is measured in terms of years. The wind whips the desiccated surface, driving sand dunes in a constantly shifting pattern so unstable as to deny all plant life the time to take root and the moisture to even germinate.

Most of the world's deserts, however, are not quite so inhospitable. In these arid but not impossibly hostile regions, the plant kingdom employs the strategy of dormancy to its ultimate limits. The seemingly desolate surroundings conceal countless millions of seeds, patiently awaiting the next wet spell to burst out, often in a fragrant and colorful carpet of flowers. The growing season is so short that it is extremely difficult for even perennial plants to survive, much less an occasional arboreal species—and yet many of them do. For example, the deserts of the American Southwest host numerous perennial cacti, including the giant saguaro (*Carnegiea gigantea*), which attain both great age and considerable height, dwarfing many fruit-producing temperate-zone cultivars. The cactus family achieves this apparent miracle, in part, by carrying the moisture-conserving strategy of succulent tissue to its extreme.

Many deserts around the world host various species of palms (*Palmae*), junipers (*Juniperus*), acacia (*Acacia* spp.), and even members of the willow family (*Salix*). These trees, more typical of wetter regions, are actually opportunistic intruders rather than species genetically adapted to desert conditions. The palms cluster around oases, forming what is actually a separate mini-biome of a decidedly wetter nature. Similarly, the junipers and other species tend to colonize sites where the drainage patterns cause runoff to accumulate in adequate amounts to keep the subsoil relatively moist.

Like other trees living in deserts, saguaro cacti (Carnegiea gigantea) conserve precious moisture by flowering only when the meager rainfall permits.

ALOE TREE / *Aloe bainesii*

The aloes are succulents; only a few members of the group grow to tree size. The largest of these is *Aloe bainesii*. It follows a distinctive branching pattern: Starting at a height of about six feet (2 m), the trunk splits in two, then each branch splits again and so on, until the branches end in clusters of dark-green, sword-shaped leaves with toothed margins. The aloe tree produces rosy, cylindrical flowers and is often planted as an ornamental. When cultivated, the trunk can grow to five feet (1.5 m) in diameter— about double its size in the wild.

Size: Grows to 60 feet (18 m) in height, with diameter of up to 5 feet (1.5 m)

Range: South Africa

SAGUARO CACTUS / *Carnegiea gigantea*

Size: From 25 to 55 feet (8 to 17 m) tall with several to many spine-covered arms

Range: Desert regions of southwestern U.S. and northern Mexico

The saguaro is the largest cactus in the United States. Seedlings grow slowly, often in the shade of paloverde trees, and first bloom when they are fifty years old. Each stem may produce hundreds of funnel-shaped, white flowers, which blossom at different times. Flowers are short-lived, opening in the late afternoon and closing the next afternoon, and pollination occurs mostly at night, carried out by bats and moths. The saguaro is home to the Gila woodpecker and the gilded flicker, which chisel out small holes in the trunk. The cactus is not harmed by the attacks: It forms a tough scab around the holes to protect itself from drying out. Native Americans used the wood for building material and fuel, and the edible fruits were considered a delicacy.

GREGG CATCLAW / *Acacia greggii*

Size: Has many spreading, thorny branches and often forms thickets from 3 to 10 feet (1 to 3 m) tall; may occur as tree up to 20 feet (6 m) tall

Range: Arid areas of southwestern U.S.

The Gregg catclaw gets its name from the short, curved spines—resembling the claws of a cat—that grow on the branches. The feathery, gray-green leaves have many small leaflets. Fragrant, creamy-yellow flowers provide an important source of nectar for honeybees. The twisted pods, up to six inches (15 cm) long, were ground into a flour by native North Americans to make bread or porridge. The Gregg catclaw requires more water than other shrubs of arid lands. It is very tolerant of fire and can recover rapidly, even after repeated burns, by sprouting from the base of the trunk.

UTAH JUNIPER / *Juniperus osteosperma*

A small, low-branching evergreen, the Utah juniper is at home in the dry, thin soils of the mesas and mountain slopes of the American Southwest and a familiar sight along the south rim of the Grand Canyon. The Utah juniper has shaggy, gray bark and scalelike leaves pressed close against the branchlets. It produces male and female cones on separate trees. The cones are small and berrylike and are edible. The Utah juniper typically grows in pure stands, but is sometimes found with other trees, including its look-alike, the oneseed juniper (*Juniperus monosperma*).

Size: Grows to 25 feet (7.5 m) tall, with diameter of 6 to 12 inches (15 to 30 cm)

Range: American Southwest between Rockies and Sierra Nevada

DATE PALM / *Phoenix dactylifera*

Size: Up to 100 feet (30 m) tall, with leaves 15 to 25 feet (5 to 7 m) long; clump of palms form if shoots at base of trunk allowed to grow

Range: From northern Africa east to India; also planted in hot, dry regions of U.S. for fruit production and in other parts of North America as ornamental

An important tree of desert oases, the date palm has been cultivated in the Middle East since at least 3000 B.C. The trunk stands tall and straight, about the same thickness all the way up, and is well protected by the bases of long-dead leaves that have fallen off. The tree is topped by a magnificent crown of large, pinnate leaves shaped like feathers. The fruits, which grow on strands that hang down in bunches from the crown of female trees, ripen from green to gold or sometimes red. Like many other palms, *Phoenix dactylifera* may be tapped to obtain a sugary sap that can be fermented to make palm wine or boiled down to provide sugar.

BLUE PALOVERDE / *Cercidium floridum*

Size: Up to 40 feet (12 m) in height with multiple stems

Range: Sonoran desert lowlands of southwestern U.S. and northwestern Mexico

The blue paloverde is well-adapted to live in arid climates. It sheds its tiny leaflets in early summer and regrows them in late summer or late fall, depending on summer rains. The name "paloverde" means "green branch" in Spanish and refers to the tree's distinctive green bark, which carries out photosynthesis. This allows the tree to obtain energy while losing minimal water through evaporation from its leaves. The paloverde flowers sporadically after spring rains, producing a dramatic bloom of long, bright-yellow clusters. Wildlife use the tree for browsing.

CALIFORNIA WASHINGTONIA / *Washingtonia filifera*

This relatively rare tree is the only palm native to western North America. It grows along desert streams and canyons in a restricted area of the American Southwest. The California Washingtonia has a thick, unbranching trunk and fan-shaped fronds edged with sharp hooks. The old, dried-out leaves often cling to the tree, hanging down and obscuring the trunk. The tree produces bunches of white, funnel-shaped flowers, followed by black, berrylike fruit, which was eaten by native North Americans fresh or dried.

Size: Grows to about 50 feet (15 m), with diameter of 12 to 48 inches (30 to 120 cm)

Range: Southwest Arizona, southeast California, and adjacent region of northern Mexico

DESERT-WILLOW / *Chilopsis linearis*

Size: Grows to 25 feet (7.5 m) in height, with diameter of about 6 inches (15 cm)

Range: Southern California, Texas, and northern Mexico

The desert-willow is the only member of its genus and is unrelated to the true willows of the family Salicaceae. It is a small deciduous tree and owes its common name to its long, slender leaves. The large white and pink flowers are sweet-smelling and resemble orchids. The brown fruit is cigar-shaped and contains many flat, winged seeds with long hairs. The slender stems of the tree are used for basketry and the wood for fuel and fence posts. Desert-willows favor old stream beds and their presence indicates that there is water just below the surface for at least part of the year.

RESOURCE GUIDE

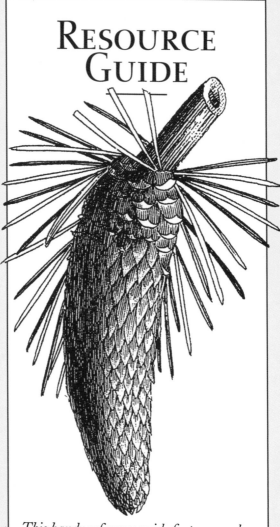

This handy reference guide features a selection of useful tree books and websites, and a chart of the state and provincial trees of the United States and Canada. On pages 178 to 179, the trees described in the third section of the book are classified according to genera. A glossary of terms is on pages 182 to 183.

Bibliography

BOOKS

1,001 Questions Answered About Trees
Rutherford Platt; Dover Publications; 1992

Balancing Act: Environmental Issues in Forestry
J.P. Kimmins, Hamish Kimmins; University of British Columbia Press; 1997

Ancient Trees: Trees that Live for 1,000 Years
Anna Lewington, Edward Parker, Anna Levington; Collins and Brown; 1999

Bonsai: Its Art, Science, History and Philosophy
Deborah R. Koreshoff; Timber Press; 1997

DK Pockets: Trees
Theresa Greenaway; DK Publishing; 1995

Encyclopedia of North American Trees Sam Benvie; Firefly Book; 2000

Eyewitness Handbooks: Trees
Allen J. Coombes, Charles A. Wills, Gillian Roberts; DK Publishing; 1992

Fantastic Trees
Edwin A. Menninger; Timber Press; 1995

A Field Guide to Eastern Trees
(*Peterson Field Guides*), George A. Petrides, Janet Wehr, Roger Tory Peterson; Houghton Mifflin Co.; 1998

A Field Guide to Western Trees
(*Peterson Field Guides*), George A. Petrides, Roger Tory Peterson; Houghton Mifflin Co.; 1998

How to Identify Trees of Britain and Europe
P. Harding, Gil Tomblin; Harper Collins; 1998

The Life of an Oak: An Intimate Portrait
Glenn Keator, Susan Bazell; Heyday Books; 1998

Manual of Woody Landscape Plants
Michael A. Dirr; Stipes Publishing; 1998

Meetings With Remarkable Trees
Thomas Pakenham; Random House; 1998

The National Audubon Society Field Guide to North American Trees: Eastern Region
Elbert L. Little; Alfred A. Knopf; 1980

The National Audubon Society Field Guide to North American Trees: Western Region
Elbert L. Little; Alfred A. Knopf; 1980

The Tree Identification Book
George Wellington, Dillingham Symonds; William Morrow and Co.; 1974

The Trees of My Forest
Bernd Heinrich; Cliff Street Books; 1997

The Trees of North America
Alan Mitchell, David More; Checkmark Books; 1987

WEBSITES

American Forests
http://www.american forests.org

British Trees
http://www.u-net. com/trees/

Database of Trees
http://www.igin.com/ treelist.html

The New York Botanical Garden
http://www.nybg.org/

Royal Botanical Gardens, Kew
http://www. rbgkew.org.uk

Ultimate Tree Ring Web Pages
http://tree.ltrr.arizona.edu/ ~grissino/henri.htm

USDA Forest Products Laboratory
http:// www.fpl.fs.fed.us/ welcome.text.html

Tree Conservation Information Service
http://www.wcmc.org.uk/ trees/

Classification of Life–Zone Trees

The third section of this book, Trees: A Life–Zone Guide (beginning on page 82), features profiles and illustrations of 161 tree species from around the world. The following list groups these trees by taxonomic class (Filicinae, Gymnosperm, and Angiosperm), then by order or subclass.

FERNS

The ferns were among the first seed-bearing plants, but the few dozen modern tree ferns that survive, some of which reach heights of more than seventy feet (21 m), all propagate by spores.

FERN

Tree fern - *Cyathea*

GYMNOSPERMS

The gymnosperms—plants with uncovered, or "naked," seeds—appeared during the Carboniferous period more than 300 million years ago. The conifers account for more than two-thirds of the surviving gymnosperm species, which also include a few modern cycads that reach tree size and one species of ginkgo.

CONIFERS

Baldcypress - *Taxodium distichum*
Cedar, Alaska - *Chamaecyparis nootkatensis*
Cedar of Lebanon - *Cedrus Libani*
Cypress, Monterey - *Cupressus macrocarpa*
Douglas-fir - *Pseudotsuga menziesii*
Fir, balsam - *Abies balsamea*
Hemlock (eastern) - *Tsuga canadensis*
Juniper, Utah - *Juniperus osteosperma*
Kauri - *Agathis australis*
Monkey-puzzle - *Araucaria araucana*
Pine, loblolly - *Pinus taeda*
Pine, lodgepole - *Pinus contorta*
Pine, longleaf - *Pinus palustris*
Pine, Ponderosa - *Pinus ponderosa*
Pine, red - *Pinus resinosa*
Pine, sugar - *Pinus lambertiana*
Pine, western white - *Pinus monticola*
Pinyon - *Pinus edulis*
Redcedar, eastern - *Juniperus virginiana*
Redwood, coast - *Sequoia sempervirens*
Redwood, dawn - *Metasequoia glyptostroboides*

Sequoia, giant - *Sequoiadendron giganteum*
Spruce, black - *Picea mariana*
Spruce, Sitka - *Picea sitchensis*
Spruce, white - *Picea glauca*
Tamarack (larch) - *Larix larcina*
White cedar- *Thuja occidentalis*

GINKGO

Ginkgo - *Ginkgo biloba*

ANGIOSPERMS

The angiosperms—plants with encased seeds, such as apple trees—first appear in the fossil record as primitive, dicot (broadleaf) trees dating back more than 100 million years ago. The dicots now dominate the world's terrestrial flora in number of tree species. The monocots more often grow as grasses and herbs, but have also produced some tree species, such as palms, bamboo, and a few tree-size lilies.

DICOTS

Albizzia - *Albizia lebbek*
Alder, red - *Alnus rubra*
Allspice - *Pimenta dioica*
Almond, Indian - *Terminalia catappa*
Annatto - *Bixa orellana*
Apple, crab - *Malus coronaria*
Ash, American - *Fraxinus americana*
Ash, American mountain - *Sorbus americana*
Ash, black - *Fraxinus nigra*
Avocado - *Persea americana*
Balsa - *Ochroma pyramidale*
Baobab - *Adansonia digitata*
Basswood, American - *Tilia americana*
Beech - *Fagus grandifolia*
Beefwood - *Casuarina equisetifolia*
Birch, paper - *Betula papyrifera*
Bottlebrush - *Callistemon spp.*
Boxelder - *Acer negundo*
Brazilnut - *Bertholletia excelsa*
Breadfruit - *Artocarpus altilis*
Butternut - *Juglans cinerea*
Cacoa - *Theobroma cacao*
Cactus, saguaro - *Carnegiea gigantea*
Calabash - *Crescentia cujete*
California-laurel - *Umbellularia californica*
Camphor-tree - *Cinnamomum camphora*
Cannonball-tree - *Couroupita guianensis*
Carambola - *Averrhoa carambola*

Cashew - *Anacardium occidentale*
Cassia - *Cassia fistula*
Catalpa, northern - *Catalpa speciosa*
Catclaw, Gregg - *Acacia greggii*
Cherimoya - *Annona cherimola*
Cherry, black - *Prunus serotina*
Chestnut, American - *Castanea dentata*
Cinnamon - *Cinnamomum verum* (also classified: *Cinnamomum zeylanicum*)
Colatree - *Cola acuminata*
Cordia - *Cordia subcordata*
Cottonwood, plains - *Populus deltoides*
Cottonwood, Fremont - *Populus fremontii*
Desert-willow - *Chilopsis linearis*
Dogwood, flowering - *Cornus florida*
Elm, American - *Ulmus americana*
Fig, common - *Ficus carica*
Fish-poison-tree - *Piscidia piscipula*
Flamboyant tree - *Delonix regia*
Guava - *Psidium guajava*
Hackberry - *Celtis occidentalis*
Hawthorn, English - *Crataegus laevigata*
Holly, English - *Ilex aquifolium*
Honeylocust - *Gleditsia triacanthos*
Hophornbeam, eastern - *Ostrya virginiana*
Horsechestnut - *Aesculus hippocastanum*
Jacaranda - *Jacaranda mimosifolia*
Jarrah - *Eucalyptus marginata*
Kapoktree - *Ceiba pentandra*
Lignumvitae - *Guaiacum officinale*
Locust, black - *Robinia pseudoacacia*
Lychee - *Litchi chinensis*
Madrone, Pacific - *Arbutus menziesii*
Magnolia, southern - *Magnolia grandiflora*
Mahogany, bigleaf - *Swietenia macrophylla*
Mango - *Mangifera indica*
Mangrove - *Rhizophora mangle*
Maple, Norway - *Acer platanoides*
Maple, red - *Acer rubrum*
Maple, silver - *Acer saccharinum*
Maple, sugar - *Acer saccharum*
Mesquite - *Prosopis juliflora*
Mulberry, red - *Morus rubra*
Nutmeg - *Myristica fragrans*
Oak, bur - *Quercus macrocarpa*
Oak, coast live - *Quercus agrifolia*
Oak, cork - *Quercus suber*
Oak, English - *Quercus robur*
Oak, red - *Quercus rubra*
Olive - *Olea europaea*
Orange, Osage - *Maclura pomifera*
Orange, sweet - *Citrus sinensis*
Orchid tree - *Bauhinia variegata*
Padauk, African - *Pterocarpus soyauxii*
Paloverde, blue - *Cercidium floridum*
Papaya - *Carica papaya*

Paulownia, royal - *Paulownia tomentosa*
Pawpaw - *Asimina triloba*
Peppertree - *Schinus molle*
Poplar, balsam - *Populus balsamifera*
Peach - *Prunus persica*
Pecan - *Carya illinoinensis*
Persimmon, common - *Diospyros virginiana*
Pistachio - *Pistacia vera*
Pomegranate - *Punica granatum*
Poplar, Lombardy - *Populus nigra* var. *italica*
Purpleheart - *Peltogyne paniculata*
Ramin - *Gonystylus bancanus*
Redbud - *Cercis canadensis*
Rubbertree - *Hevea brasiliensis*
Russian-olive - *Elaeagnus angustifolia*
Saltree - *Shorea robusta*
Sandalwood - *Santalum album*
Sapodilla - *Manilkara zapota*
Sandbox tree - *Hura crepitans*
Sassafras - *Sassafras albidum*
Sausage tree - *Kigelia pinnata*
Sea grape - *Coccoloba uvifera*
Silky-oak - *Grevillea robusta*
Smoketree, American - *Cotinus obovatus*
Spanish-cedar - *Cedrela odorata*
Sumac, staghorn - *Rhus typhina*
Sycamore - *Platanus occidentalis*
Tamarind - *Tamarindus indica*
Tanoak - *Lithocarpus densiflorus*
Tupelo, black - *Nyssa sylvatica*
Tupelo, water - *Nyssa aquatica*
Teak - *Tectona grandis*
Tree-of-heaven - *Ailanthus altissima*
Tulip tree, African - *Spathodea campanulata*
Walnut, black - *Juglans nigra*
Wattle, black - *Acacia mearnsii*
Willow, Babylon weeping - *Salix babylonica*
Willow, black - *Salix nigra*
Yellow-poplar - *Liriodendron tulipifera*
Zebrawood - *Microberlinia brazzavillensis*

MONOCOTS

Aloe tree - *Aloe bainesii*
California Washingtonia - *Washingtonia filifera*
Coconut palm - *Cocos nucifera*
Dragontree - *Dracaena draco* (Canary Islands)
Palm, date - *Phoenix dactylifera*
Palm, latan - *Latania loddigesii*
Palm, royal - *Roystonea regia* (West Indies)
Pine, screw - *Pandanus tectorius*
Traveler's-tree - *Ravenala madagascariensis*

Official Trees (U.S./Canada)

OFFICIAL TREES OF THE UNITED STATES

STATE	COMMON NAME/LATIN NAME	YEAR DESIGNATED
ALABAMA:	LONGLEAF PINE (PINUS PALUSTRIS)	1949
ALASKA:	SITKA SPRUCE (PICEA SITCHENSIS)	1962
ARIZONA:	PALOVERDE (CERCIDIUM FLORIDUM)	1945
ARKANSAS:	SHORTLEAF PINE (PINUS ECHINATA)	1939
CALIFORNIA:	COAST REDWOOD (SEQUOIA SEMPERVIRENS)	1937
	GIANT SEQUOIA (SEQUOIADENDRON GIGANTEUM)	1953
COLORADO:	BLUE SPRUCE (PICEA PUNGENS)	1939
CONNECTICUT:	WHITE OAK (QUERCUS ALBA)	1947
DELAWARE:	AMERICAN HOLLY (ILEX OPACA)	1939
FLORIDA:	CABBAGE PALMETTO (SABAL PALMETTO)	1953
GEORGIA:	LIVE OAK (QUERCUS VIRGINIANA)	1937
HAWAII:	KUKUI/CANDLENUT (ALEURITES)	1959
IDAHO:	WESTERN WHITE PINE (PINUS MONTICOLA)	1935
ILLINOIS:	WHITE OAK (QUERCUS ALBA)	1973
INDIANA:	YELLOW-POPLAR (LIRIODENDRON TULIPIFERA)	1931
IOWA:	OAK (QUERCUS SPP)	1961
KANSAS:	EASTERN COTTONWOOD (POPULUS DELTOIDES)	1937
KENTUCKY:	KENTUCKY COFFEE TREE (GYMNOCLADUS DIOICA)	1937
LOUISIANA:	BALDCYPRESS (TAXODIUM DISTICHUM)	1963
MAINE:	EASTERN WHITE PINE (PINUS STROBUS)	1945
MARYLAND:	WHITE OAK (QUERCUS ALBA)	1941
MASSACHUSETTS:	AMERICAN ELM (ULMUS AMERICANA)	1941
MICHIGAN:	EASTERN WHITE PINE (PINUS STROBUS)	1955
MINNESOTA:	RED PINE (PINUS RESINOSA)	1953
MISSISSIPPI:	SOUTHERN MAGNOLIA (MAGNOLIA GRANDIFLORA)	1938
MONTANA:	PONDEROSA PINE (PINUS PONDEROSA)	1949
NEBRASKA:	EASTERN COTTONWOOD (POPULUS DELTOIDES)	1972
NEVADA:	SINGLE-LEAF PINYON (PINUS MONOPHYLLA)	1959
	BRISTLECONE PINE (PINUS ARISTATA)	1987
NEW HAMPSHIRE:	PAPER BIRCH (BETULA PAPYRIFERA)	1947
NEW JERSEY:	RED OAK (QUERCUS RUBRA)	1950
NEW MEXICO:	PINYON (PINUS EDULIS)	1949

OFFICIAL TREES OF THE UNITED STATES (CONTINUED)

STATE	COMMON NAME/LATIN NAME	YEAR DESIGNATED
NEW YORK:	SUGAR MAPLE (ACER SACCHARUM)	1956
NORTH CAROLINA:	LONGLEAF PINE (PINUS PALUSTRIS)	1963
NORTH DAKOTA:	AMERICAN ELM (ULMUS AMERICANA)	1947
OHIO:	OHIO BUCKEYE (AESCULUS GLABRA)	1953
OKLAHOMA:	REDBUD (CERCIS CANADENSIS)	1937
OREGON:	DOUGLAS-FIR (PSEUDOTSUGA MENZIESII)	1939
PENNSYLVANIA:	EASTERN HEMLOCK (TSUGA CANADENSIS)	1931
RHODE ISLAND:	RED MAPLE (ACER RUBRUM)	1964
SOUTH CAROLINA:	CABBAGE PALMETTO (SABAL PALMETTO)	1939
SOUTH DAKOTA:	WHITE SPRUCE (PICEA GLAUCA)	1947
TENNESSEE:	YELLOW-POPLAR (LIRIODENDRON TULIPIFERA)	1947
TEXAS:	PECAN (CARYA ILLINOINENSIS)	1947
UTAH:	BLUE SPRUCE (PICEA PUNGENS)	1933
VERMONT:	SUGAR MAPLE (ACER SACCHARUM)	1949
VIRGINIA:	FLOWERING DOGWOOD (CORNUS FLORIDA)	1956
WASHINGTON:	WESTERN HEMLOCK (TSUGA HETEROPHYLLA)	1947
WEST VIRGINIA:	SUGAR MAPLE (ACER SACCHARUM)	1949
WISCONSIN:	SUGAR MAPLE (ACER SACCHARINUM)	1949
WYOMING:	PLAINS COTTONWOOD (POPULUS SARGENTII)	1947

OFFICIAL TREES OF CANADA

PROVINCE	COMMON NAME/LATIN NAME	YEAR DESIGNATED
ALBERTA:	LODGEPOLE PINE (PINUS LATIFOLIA)	1984
BRITISH COLUMBIA:	WESTERN REDCEDAR (THUJA PLICATA)	1988
MANITOBA:	WHITE SPRUCE (PICEA GLAUCA)	1987
NEW BRUNSWICK:	BALSAM FIR (ABIES BALSAMEA)	1987
NEWFOUNDLAND:	BLACK SPRUCE (PICEA MARIANA)	1993
NORTHWEST TERRITORIES:	JACK PINE (PINUS BANKSIANA)	1990
NOVA SCOTIA:	RED SPRUCE (PICEA RUGENS)	1987
ONTARIO:	EASTERN WHITE PINE (PINUS STROBUS)	1984
PRINCE EDWARD ISLAND:	RED OAK (QUERCUS RUBRA)	1987
QUEBEC:	YELLOW BIRCH (BETULA ALLEGHANIENSIS)	1993
SASKATCHEWAN:	PAPER BIRCH (BETULA PAPYRIFERA)	1988

Glossary

Angiosperm: A flowering plant or tree, such as the apple tree, the seeds of which are enclosed by an ovary. Broad-leaved trees and palm trees are angiosperms.

Berry: A small fleshy fruit, often brightly colored, that contains many seeds.

Bisexual: A plant or tree with flowers that bear both male and female reproductive organs in the same flower. A hermaphrodite.

Blade: The expanded section of a leaf.

Bole: The section of a trunk that extends from the lowest branches of the tree down to the root flare, where the trunk begins to splay outward.

Bract: A specialized leaf, often blade-shaped or scalelike.

Broad-leaved trees: Angiosperm tree species belonging to the subgroup known as Dicotyledonae.

Cambium: An active layer of cells below the bark that lines the trunk, branches, roots, and stems of a tree or plant. Cells in the cambium layer divide inward to form xylem and outward to form phloem.

Capsule: A simple, dry fruit that usually splits open to release the seeds it contains.

Catkin: Stalkless flowers that hang in long, narrow clusters in certain trees; named for their resemblance to cat tails.

Chaparral: A biome with moist summers and dry winters, where shrubby trees dominate.

Clone: A group of plants that have been propagated asexually from a parent plant and therefore shares the same genetic makeup.

Compound leaf: A leaf that is composed of separate blades or leaflets.

Cone-scale: The flat, overlapping structure that bears the seeds in the female cones of certain conifers.

Cone: The reproductive structure—both male and female—of conifers. Male cones are composed of groups of pollen sacs and are short-lived. Female cones bear "naked" egg-containing ovules on their surfaces. Female cones become woody after fertilization.

Conifer: A tree that bears cones.

Cork: A protective layer of dead cells on the surface of a stem, trunk, or root.

Cotyledon: The first leaves to develop inside a seed's embryo. Monocots have one cotyledon, dicots have two, and conifers may have more than ten in each embryo.

Cryptogram: A type of plant that does not produce seeds.

Cultivar: A cultivated plant that has been selected for its ornamental qualities or some other use. Cultivars are often hybrids or genetic variants that do not appear outside of cultivation.

Cuticle: The impermeable outer layer of a leaf's epidermis that protects and prevents water loss.

Dicotyledon: One of two subclasses of angiosperms; includes broad-leaved trees. Also called dicot.

Dimorphic: Having two distinct forms.

Deciduous: A tree that sheds its leaves during a single season.

Earlywood: Wood produced by a tree early in the growing season. Earlywood is characterized by large cells with thin walls and is often light colored.

Ecotone: A transitional area of vegetation between two major vegetation types, such as forest and grassland.

Entire: A smooth-edged leaf.

Epidermis: The leaf's protective layer just below the cuticle.

Flower: The structure involved in a tree's sexual reproduction. Flowers usually have either male or female organs, although some are bisexual.

Fruit: The ripened ovary of a seed plant and its contents, including the ripened seeds.

Genus: A taxonomic rank for a group of related plants, which is divided into several subordinate species.

Growth ring: The area of growth by which a tree increases in diameter every year; comprised of earlywood and latewood.

Gymnosperm: Plant or tree species, such as conifers, the seeds of which are not enclosed in an ovary (fruit or nut).

Imbricate: Petals or sepals that overlap.

Inflorescence: A cluster of flowers growing from a single stalk.

Latewood: Wood produced by a tree late in the growing season; characterized by small, thick-walled cells and is often darker than earlywood.

Leaflet: A single division of a compound leaf.

Lenticel: The porelike openings in bark used in gaseous exchange.

Lobe: A protruding section of a leaf.

Mesophyll: The tissues inside a leaf involved in photosynthesis.

Montane: A mountain-forest zone.

Monocotyledon: One of two subclasses of angiosperms; includes palm trees. Also called monocot.

Needle: A long, narrow needlelike leaf.

Nut: A single-seed fruit that is partially or fully encased in a tough, dry husk or shell.

Ovary: The part of the flower that contains the ovule.

Ovule: The structure in a flower or cone that, once fertilized, develops into the embryo.

Phloem: Vascular tissue in the inner bark that transports food material made by the plant.

Photosynthesis: The process through which a plant synthesizes carbohydrates from carbon dioxide and water by using sunlight and chlorophyll.

Pollen: The collective term for pollen grains: microscopic grains produced by flowers that contain genetic information needed for the sexual reproduction of plants and trees.

Pollination: The transfer of pollen from male to female flowers for the purposes of sexual reproduction.

Polygamous: Having both bisexual and male or female flowers on the same plant.

Savanna: Grasslands with a scattering of individual trees or stands of trees.

Scale: A small, stiff, reduced leaf.

Shrub: A woody perennial plant less than ten feet in height. Distinguished from a tree by having low side branches instead of a main trunk.

Simple: Leaves that are not divided into leaflets.

Species: The basic unit of classification.

Stomata: Microscopic valvelike openings on a leaf (usually on the underside) used for gaseous exchange.

Stomatal bands: Light-colored areas on a leaf indicating a high density of stomata.

Xylem: Basic wood tissue in the inner bark composed of long, thick-walled cells that transports water and mineral salts through the tree.

Index

Text references are in plain type; illustrations in *italic;* photographs in **bold**; tree profiles in *italic* with asterisk (*).

ST. REMY MEDIA

President: Pierre Léveillé
Vice-President, Finance: Natalie Watanabe
Managing Editor: Carolyn Jackson
Managing Art Director: Diane Denoncourt
Production Manager: Michelle Turbide
Director, Business Development: Christopher Jackson
Senior Editor: Pierre Home-Douglas
Art Director: Robert Paquet
Associate Editor: Ned Meredith
Writers: Jon Arno, Stacey Berman, Jennifer Ormston, Daniel Schneider, Silvija Ulmanis
Species' Profile Writers: Helen Fyles, Rebecca Smollett
Researchers: Jessica Braun, Heather Mills
Illustrators: Stephen Aitken, Monique Chaussé, Patrick Jougla, Jiyoung Lee, Rosemarie Schwab
Photo Researcher: Linda Castle
Indexer: Linda Cardella Cournoyer
Senior Editor, Production: Brian Parsons
Systems Director: Edward Renaud
Technical Support: Joey Fraser, Jean Sirois
Scanner Operator: Martin Francoeur

The following persons also assisted in the preparation of this book:
Robert Chartier, Lorraine Doré, Dominique Gagné, and Solange Laberge.

ACKNOWLEDGMENTS

The editors wish to thank the following:
Alton Arakaki and Rogerene Arce, Cooperative Extension Service, University of Hawaii at Manoa, Hoolehua, HI; George Constable, for his editorial contributions; Mihaly Czako, Ph.D., Department of Biological Sciences, University of South Carolina, Columbia, SC; Thelma Krug, Coordinator for Earth Observation, Institute Nacional de Pesquiais, Sao Jose dos Campos, Brazil; the library and médiathéque staff at the Montreal Botanical Gardens, Montreal, Quebec; Carrie Tome, Dr. Joe Woodrow, and Dr. Ken Grace, University of Hawaii at Manoa, Honolulu, HI; Lynka Woodbury, Fairchild Tropical Garden, Miami, FL.

PICTURE CREDITS

Eastcott/Momatiuk/Earth Scenes-4 (upper left), 6-7, 25 (lower); John Shaw/Auscape-8; Peter French/Bruce Coleman Inc.-9; Kent & Donna Dannen/Photo Researchers, Inc.-10 ; Jaime Plaza Van Roon/Auscape-11; Lawrence Naylor/Photo Researchers, Inc.-13; Volker Steger/Science Photo Library/Photo Researchers, Inc.-4 (upper right), 14; Jack Wilburn/Earth Scenes-15; Jim Zipp/Photo Researchers, Inc.-18; Merlin D. Tuttle/Bat Conservation International/Photo Researchers, Inc.-19; Don Enger/Animals Animals-20; Rolf Kopfle/Bruce Coleman Inc.-21; Nils Reinhard/OKAPIA/Photo Researchers, Inc.-22; Phil Degginger/Earth Scenes-23; Taylor, H. OSF/Earth Scenes-4 (lower right), 24; Wendell Metzen/Bruce Coleman Inc.-25 (upper); Andrew Syred/Science Photo Library/Photo Researchers, Inc.-26; John Kaprielian/Photo Researchers, Inc.-28; George Ranalli/Photo Researchers, Inc.-29; Richard Reid / Earth Scenes-30; Joyce Burek/Earth Scenes-31; John Lemker/Earth Scenes-33; Kerry T. Givens/Bruce Coleman Inc.-34; Ken Eward/Science Source/Photo Researchers, Inc.-35; Bruce Coleman Inc.-36; Robert P. Carr/Bruce Coleman Inc.-38; Kathie.Atkinson/Auscape-39; Kenneth W. Fink/Photo Researchers, Inc.-40; M.P. Kahl/Bruce Coleman Inc.-41; Bates Littlehales/Earth Scenes-42; Francois Gohier/Photo Researchers, Inc.-43 (upper); Jean Claude Carton/Bruce Coleman Inc.-43 (lower); Frank Oberle Photography/Bruce Coleman Inc.-44; Mary Evans Picture Library-45; Jean-Loup Charmet/Science Photo Library/Photo Researchers, Inc.-46; Arthur Beck/Photo Researchers, Inc.-5 (lower right), 47; Gregory K. Scott/Photo Researchers, Inc. -48; S. Michael Bisceglie/Earth Scenes-49; Nigel J. H. Smith/Earth Scenes-51; Holt Studios Int/Photo Researchers, Inc.-52; Finnish Forest Tree Breeding-53; Hans Reinhard/Bruce Coleman Inc.-54; Georg Gerster/Photo Researchers, Inc.-55; Richard Walker/Bruce Coleman Inc.-56; Adrian Davies/Bruce Coleman Inc.-57; John Mead/Science Photo Library/Photo Researchers, Inc.-58; Dominic Sansoni/Auscape-59; Dr. Morley Read/Science Photo Library/Photo Researchers, Inc.-60; Christine M. Douglas/Photo Researchers, Inc.-61; Jack W. Dykinga/Bruce Coleman Inc.-62; John Shaw/Bruce Coleman Inc.-63, 172; Deni McIntyre/Photo Researchers, Inc.-64; John Elk III/Bruce Coleman Inc.-65, 160; Geospace/Science Photo Library/Photo Researchers, Inc.-66; F. Stuart Westmorland/Source/ Photo Researchers, Inc.-5 (upper left), 68-69; Robert Chartier-70, 78, 79; Renee Lynn/Photo Researchers, Inc.-80; Bob Burch/Bruce Coleman Inc.-81; Hans Reinhard/OKAPIA/Photo Researchers, Inc.-5 (lower left), 82-83; Doug Wechsler/Earth Scenes-86; Tom McHugh/Photo Researchers, Inc.-121; Aaron Haupt/ Photo Researchers, Inc.-140; Ferrero-Labat/Auscape-151; Jeff Foott/Auscape-166.